# 21
## DAYS
### TO SUCCESS
*Through*

# NETWORKING

# What People Are Saying About
## *21 Days to Success Through Networking*

"Sukenick and Williams have mastered the art and science of one of the most sought marketing tools in the 21st century. It's amazing to watch Gnik as he builds a solid network of contacts in only 21 days. This is a book I'm sharing with everyone, every day, all year long."
> —Steve Bono, presidential director, Lightyear Wireless

"Shows you how to go about creating strong relationships and healthy networks, which ultimately can lead to great success. ... A solid addition to any networking library."
> —Susan Baroncini-Moe, author, *Business in Blue Jeans: How to Have a Successful Business on Your Own Terms, in Your Own Style*

"A must read—Sukenick and Williams will show you how to become a master networker as you read their fascinating story of networking success. I know this book will be one you refer to over and over again."
> —Andrea Nierenberg, author, *Savvy Networking: 118 Fast and Effective Tips for Business Success*

"This book makes it easy to comprehend the commonly overlooked values of networking success. The networking fundamentals I have learned from this book will serve me for the rest of my career. ... *21 Days to Success Through Networking* is the perfect balance of fun and informative reading."
> —Sara Deuser, database coordinator and finance assistant, National Precast Concrete Association

"I am embarking on a new adventure like Gnik and found Gnik's 'Aha!' moments insightful and important. The story allows the concepts to be well defined, easily understood, and enjoyable. I like the simplicity of the ideas and took notes so I can remember what to do. Great read!"
> —Dawn Davis, special education teacher, Davis School District (UT)

"Thought you would like to know your book just helped me at work. 'What others have to say is more important than what I have to say.' I just got bonus points with my boss. Thanks!"
> —Abigail Stearns, personal banker, Chase Bank

"Sukenick and Williams brilliantly craft the tale of Gnik Rowten, a person just like you or me, who, when about to start the next chapter of his life, rises to the occasion with the help of a few new friends in just 21 days—the time it takes for one to develop a new habit. Whether you've already been on a journey such as Gnik's or are embarking on one for your very first time, read this book."

—Adam J. Kovitz, founder and CEO, #KESocial

"It is a quick and easy read. It's a good book and I totally like the ideas and the teaching that you are doing through your characters."

—Jeff French, service missionary, Philippines

"An inspiring read with many applicable and tangible take-away lessons."

—Beth Austin, future executive senior sales director

"I am always amazed by Ron and Ken, and their boundless energy, connecting with people and making their time and lives better. After the first paragraph of the manuscript, I lost myself in the story, coming up for air at each 'Aha!' moment."

—Rich Tensmeyer, project engineer and
data manager, Clarke Engineering

"This book instantly changed the way I approach social interactions."

—Jake Dorris, ramp agent, FedEx Express

"Loved the book. It was an enjoyable read and pulled me in because it's real and believable. Some great ideas for improving relationships both business and personal."

—Annette Dalton, hair stylist and
home-school mom, Mechanicsville, VA

"Sukenick and Williams have captured what it takes to be a master networker ... a must-read for anyone looking to be a better and more intentional connector."

—Phil Gerbyshak, chief connections officer, Milwaukee Social Media

"[This book] completely changed the way I look at and approach networking and making connections with people. Gnik (with a 'G') showed that the entire process is supposed to be easy and genuine, and more importantly, he showed me how to do it myself."

—Mark Williams, national sales trainer, ZAGG

# 21 DAYS
## TO SUCCESS
### *Through*
# NETWORKING

## The Life and Times of Gnik Rowten

Ron Sukenick and Ken Williams

CyberAge Books

Information Today, Inc.

Medford, New Jersey

*First Printing, October 2013*

*21 Days to Success Through Networking: The Life and Times of Gnik Rowten*

**Publisher's Note:** The authors and publisher have taken care in preparation of this book but make no expressed or implied warranty of any kind and assume no responsibility for errors or omissions. No liability is assumed for incidental or consequential damages in connection with or arising out of the use of the information or programs contained herein.

### Library of Congress Cataloging-in-Publication Data

Sukenick, Ron.
   21 days to success through networking : the life and times of Gnik Rowten / by Ron Sukenick and Ken Williams.
     pages cm
   ISBN 978-1-937290-03-0
   1. Business networks. 2. Social interaction. 3. Listening. I. Williams, Ken, 1968- II. Title. III. Title: Twenty one days to success through networking.
   HD69.S8S8495 2013
   650.1'3--dc23

                           2013017170

Printed and bound in the United States of America.

President and CEO: Thomas H. Hogan, Sr.
Editor-in-Chief and Publisher: John B. Bryans
VP Graphics and Production: M. Heide Dengler
Managing Editor: Amy M. Reeve
Editorial Assistant: Brandi Scardilli
Cover Designer: Lisa Conroy

Images of Gnik Rowten and Pam created by Kim Sharpe (facebook.com/kimmortal1)

**infotoday.com**

*This book is dedicated to all the people who have ever taken the time to help others in need and to friends we have met along the road. We hope you agree that there's a little bit of Gnik in each of us.*

# Contents

# Acknowledgments

Ron approached me several months ago with an idea about writing a story. "What if," he excitedly explained, "we could share the basic principles of building a network through a story? Let's make it easy for anyone to learn what to do."

I have listened to Ron teach about networking, and if anyone knows how to do it, he does. I was hooked on the idea, and we got started. The ideas started coming, and the story, piece by piece, came together. "Twenty-one days" became the theme. If one practices something for 21 days, conventional wisdom says that the behavior becomes a habit. The idea was exciting, and people whom we met shared our enthusiasm. Then Ron met John Bryans, editor-in-chief and publisher of the Books Division of Information Today, Inc. John was intrigued. We began to see that our idea might become reality.

In addition to the tremendous editorial and moral support we've received from John and his staff, we are blessed to have had access to the keen insights and the talented eye of Ariane Cagle of Cagle Multimedia (caglemultimedia.com). Ariane crystallized the concepts, making them clearer without changing Gnik's voice or personality.

Then we decided that Gnik should have a face. We found a lot of ideas that didn't completely capture the look we had imagined, but Kim Sharpe of CodeKIM3D (codeKim3D.blog spot.com) nailed it. She has done a phenomenal job of giving Gnik and Pam the look that was in our heads but we couldn't get out.

Many friends have shared feedback and expressed enthusiasm for the project. Thanks to all of you. If you're reading this, wondering if you're one of the ones who made a difference, yes, you are.

Finally, we both have very supportive families who have given us time and space to map out Gnik's journey in a new city. Thanks, Yvonne Sukenick and Marcene Williams, for your patience and gentle pressure to get things done. And thanks to Christine and Freedom, and to Allison, Brendan, Carissa, Dallton, and Eddison, for giving us reasons for being better than we thought possible.

—Ken Williams

# Prologue

The familiarity of the coffee shop was surreal. Two weeks ago, Gnik had met with his manager and handed her the short resignation letter that he had drafted more than six months before. He had left the date blank, but he knew that someday he would have to scratch the itch he had been feeling to start his own company.

> Molly,
>
> Please accept this letter as formal notification that I am resigning my position as marketing support associate, effective two weeks from today. The past 18 months have provided me with an education and development experiences that will have lasting effects on my career. Thank you for the role you

have played in my professional development. Please let me know how I can be of assistance during this transition.

Sincerely,
Gnik Rowten

He had finished his good-byes at work, and the reality of his upcoming transition was looming. Gnik would be moving away in just two days; ordinarily, he would have preferred to stay at home and keep packing, but "The Crew," as they called themselves, insisted on getting together to say their good-byes to Gnik. The Crew, Gnik's best college friends, had hung around together since they were freshmen. *This seems so weird*, Gnik thought. *Things won't ever be the same.*

Gnik was the first to arrive, and he staked out a table in the back corner of the shop. Foot traffic was light, and Gnik was certain The Crew would be able to reminisce without interruptions.

As Gnik sipped his coffee, he welcomed the surge of caffeine. He hadn't finished half his beverage before The Crew had finished gathering. The chatter of old friends reconnecting fell into a natural lull, and Chad, the group's unofficial spokesman, spoke to everyone present.

"Thanks for making time in your schedules to give Gnik a proper send-off." He turned to Gnik. "So, buddy, are you excited to be moving on to bigger and better things?"

Gnik forced a smile and faced the center of the table. "I'm a little freaked out, actually. I've been on autopilot since I decided to move. I feel like there's something big ... something important waiting for me in the city. But I don't know *what* I was thinking. I don't know anyone there. I don't have a job to go to. I have no idea what I'm doing! What the *bleep* was I thinking?"

Excited murmurings rumbled around the table as the group shifted in their seats, giving Gnik their full energy and support.

Chad sat down and motioned to Gnik. "I wish I had the guts to follow my dreams like you do. You'll be amazing."

Gnik closed his eyes, absorbing the positive vibes from his friends. Transported in time to some future moment when he would have the work and new experiences he desired, his eyes shot open, and he got serious. "There's nothing special about me. If I can do this, there's no reason you can't, too."

In unison, everyone around the table nodded. Chad spoke for all. "Maybe you're right. Maybe ..."

Gnik pointed at the people around the table. "Okay, I'll tell you what I think. First, I appreciate the confidence you have in me. That will help when I'm having a rough day. But I'm not going to let you get away with wimping out on yourselves."

His gaze focused, and his seriousness intensified. "I'll go and represent you guys. I'll figure it out, by trial and error. And when I figure it out, we'll get back together, and I'll teach you what I've learned. I can't let you give up on yourselves. We're supposed to change the world, right?"

Gnik's former college classmates looked at him in anticipation. Chad again spoke for the group. "Deal. Don't forget about us when you're rich and famous."

Others in the group piped in with their own words of wisdom.

"It's not what you know—it's *who* you know!"

"It's all about networking!"

"It's all about *people!*"

"Okay, okay," Gnik laughed. "I got it. When I get to the city, I'll start working on my network. Don't forget, though—we're all in this together. We're all on Facebook, so I expect us all to stay in touch. Plus, I'll post regular updates on Facebook or my blog, and I expect you to follow me."

The Crew joked with each other and encouraged Gnik until the barista good naturedly invited them to let him close for the night. Gnik returned home to continue packing. For the first time in days, he felt confident that moving was the right choice.

*And as with all good things in life, we will start at the beginning ...*

# day 1

# The Gift Is In the Giving

Gnik woke up after a restful night of sleep. He had arrived at his new apartment late in the afternoon the day before. He had unpacked his few belongings, making his tiny place seem more like home. He posted a quick status update to Facebook to let his friends know he had made it to his new home without incident. *First day in the city. I feel like a blank slate. Bring it on!*

Living away from home and friends for the first time, Gnik stopped at the first coffee shop he saw as his new venture dawned. He smiled to himself. He knew no one there, so he decided to make the best of the situation. A woman, probably a few years older than Gnik, was poring over charts on her iPad; conveniently, a couple of empty chairs surrounded the table where she sat. The black plastic chair directly across from her was lighter than it looked, and when Gnik pulled it back, it almost fell over.

"Excuse me," he began. "Do you mind if I sit here?" The woman nodded without looking up. "Hi. My name is Gnik with a G."

"I'm sorry?" She looked up.

Gnik smiled. "Gnik with a G. What's your name?"

The young woman seemed confused but not irritated at the interruption. "I'm Pam. Pam with a P." She smiled at her joke and took Gnik's outstretched hand, shaking it firmly. Pam noticed the notebooks and the laptop he was carrying. "Nice to meet you, Gnik with a G. And I have to ask about your name. Gnik with a G? Tell me about that."

Gnik prefaced the explanation by noting his father's tendency to "enhance" the facts of his stories. Frankly, Gnik wasn't sure he knew the hard, cold facts.

"Before my parents married, they were quite the socialites. In fact, they first met at a chamber meeting and have continued to be actively involved in various causes and networks. They found that meeting and connecting with people was a lot of fun, and they met some wonderful people as a result."

"So, where did 'Gnik' come from? Did they lose a bet?"

"Apparently, Mom and Dad went to a charity benefit after a particularly stressful week. My father indulged in the sweets— tortes, cakes, truffles, and other treats. He was standing behind the banner over the desserts table, when he looked up and laughed, because the banner read 'Stressed.'

"So, there he was. Stressed and eating desserts, when he realized that 'stressed' spelled backward is 'desserts.' My mom saw him laughing, and after that they started spelling lots of things backward to see what they got.

"At a church event, they were taught to beware of keeping their 'reward' in a 'drawer.' That got them thinking about our last name, Rowten. And then they realized if they called me 'Gnik' my name would be 'networking' spelled backwards. So, the name stuck. I'm not sure how much I believe it, but that's the story I've been told. The thing is, it's been a great way for me to break the ice when I meet people." He winked. "It worked, didn't it?"

Pam chuckled. "Yeah, I have to admit that it's a great way to start a conversation. It snapped me right out of my zombie zone. So, Gnik with a G, what do you do?"

Gnik swallowed hard. *I have a pretty good idea what I want to do, but I don't do anything yet. That's why I've moved here—to get a new start. How can I answer that question without sounding like a loser?*

Gnik decided to just dive in, be honest about his situation, and see where it led. He explained to Pam that he'd moved here to make a new start, and, while he hadn't completely ruled anything out, he was thinking about starting a marketing firm. "I've been a marketing support associate for the past year and a half, and I have a pretty good feel for the industry. For a while, now, I've been gathering information to set out on my own." As he shared what he'd done before the move and how it had turned out to be a dead end, he realized the conversation was becoming very one-sided and stopped talking abruptly.

"Gnik," Pam started, smiling knowingly. She reached across the table and touched one of Gnik's notepads. "I understand how you're feeling. Can I give you some feedback?"

Gnik felt an uncomfortable knot forming in his stomach but nodded for Pam to continue.

"The only person who knows what you want is you. The only person who knows who you really are is you. You're just like me and everyone else in this city. We all want to be someone. We all want to have something. But guess what's different between you and them?"

Gnik sat back and closed his eyes, pensively. He didn't understand Pam's riddle.

Pam continued, "If you look for it, you'll see a lot of people who are clawing their way to the top. Lots of people will step on your or my or anyone else's toes to get to where they think they should be. But not you. No, you're different."

A smile crept across Gnik's face. "I am? Yeah. I am. But … *how* am I different?"

"Let me ask you a question," Pam said. "I snuck a look as you ordered your coffee, and I noticed what you dropped into the barista's tip jar. Most people I watch will drop their change into the jar—if they give anything. But not you. You reached into your pocket for a bill. Why?"

Gnik's face began to flush, and his cheeks grew warm. "I don't know. I guess I wanted to show a little appreciation to a guy who seems to be working hard for a living."

"And," Pam said, slowly, "think about how you felt after dropping the tip into the jar. Remember, I saw the whole thing."

"What do you mean?"

"You did something unexpected and very nice for someone you didn't know. Think. How did you feel?"

Gnik grew more embarrassed. He mumbled, "It felt good."

Gnik shifted in his seat while Pam began to gather her belongings. As he looked into her eyes, Gnik felt more confident. "Good. It felt good."

## I gave because it felt good to give.

Pam stood up and apologized. "I'm sorry—I just realized I'm running late for a meeting. But think about that. Think about what you got out of giving the barista a generous tip. I hope we can continue this conversation soon. I'm here almost every morning." To reinforce her desire to reconnect, Pam dropped her business card on the table.

Gnik politely stood as Pam left. He pondered Pam's parting words. *What did I get out of that? Was I truly selfless by giving that tip? Or did I expect something more?* He felt like he was on the brink of something significant, but it seemed so simple. *I gave because it felt good to give.*

# Gnik's Aha!

The act of giving is its own reward. Giving, itself, is a gift to the giver. I can give time, assistance, energy, and resources without the expectation of anything in return.

day **2**

# What Goes Around Comes Around

Friends and family:

A quick blog post, as promised. I've been here a couple of days, and things are going well. I got settled in my apartment, and anyone who decides to visit, I'm happy to show you around. I'm right in the middle of downtown, and the view from my kitchen window is absolutely fabulous! I love just sitting and looking out over the bustling activity of the city below—especially at night, when the streets are lit up. I can see the silhouetted skyline against the black sky. In an odd way, it calms me.

I met an interesting person yesterday. I went to grab a cup of coffee, and I saw someone in the shop who I was drawn to. I can't really explain it. She was busy, but before I could talk myself out of it, I just went up and sat down at the same table. We had a great conversation. She pointed out a few things that really got me thinking. I've had some time to think about what she said, and I'll give you a quick run-down. Basically, she pointed out that when I do something nice for someone else, the good feeling I get is my payoff. It made me remember buying donuts for my high school biology teacher, hoping to bribe her to postpone a quiz. I felt a bit frustrated when it didn't work. But what Pam, the woman I met yesterday, said really makes sense. If I enjoy the moment, giving to give, sharing to share, without expecting anything in return, I end up feeling—no, I end up *being* blessed. I plan to run into Pam again. I have to thank her for her insight. Maybe, somehow, I can return the favor.

## When I do something nice for someone else, the good feeling I get is my payoff.

Gnik pressed the Publish button, smiling as he replayed yesterday's conversation with Pam in his head. He gathered his laptop and a notepad, stuffing them into his backpack, and stepped into the narrow hallway. He wasn't exactly sure where the library was, but the flyer he had seen in the coffee shop earlier had an address that seemed to be fairly close by.

There was a forum for local businesses scheduled for the afternoon, and the presentation Gnik was most interested in was called "What No One Ever Told You About Marketing." He thought it sounded relevant to the small business he was contemplating, and he wanted to learn what other small business owners needed in their own marketing.

Gnik began walking in the general direction of the library, confident that if he couldn't find it on his own he'd run into someone who could direct him. Suddenly, across the street, he saw a young man, probably a few years older than himself, scratching his head and looking confused. Gnik waited for traffic to pass, then navigated his way across the intersection to see if he could somehow help. As he drew closer, Gnik realized the man was looking at a flat tire with a puzzled expression on his face.

Confidently, Gnik asked, "Need a hand?"

"I've never changed a tire before, but I should be able to manage," the man said, clearly embarrassed. "Thanks anyway."

"I'll be happy to help."

Gnik was still charged from yesterday's conversation with Pam. He was excited about the prospect of giving himself the gift of giving. He examined the available tools and asked, "Do you have a jack?"

"I have no idea what I have." The man averted his eyes and busied himself looking through the trunk of the car.

Gnik slipped beside the man and offered, "Let me take a look."

As he pulled the flimsy cardboard cover off the spare tire well in the trunk, Gnik spotted a jack wrapped around the bolt that held the spare tire down. "Here it is. Let me show you."

Gnik showed the man how the jack worked and the position it needed to be in to safely lift the car. Together, they removed the lug nuts and the flat, then placed the spare on the bare hub. They replaced and tightened the lugs, lowered the car, and stowed the jack and flat tire in the trunk.

The man reached out to shake Gnik's hand. "Thanks so much for your time," he said and reached for his wallet. "Please, how much do I owe you for your help?"

Surprised at the offer, Gnik smiled and waved his hand. "No, it was my pleasure. Really. You don't owe me anything. But if you can tell me where the library is, that would be great."

The man offered Gnik a ride, dropping him off at the library a few minutes before the session was to begin. Gnik thanked the man for the ride, and the two shook hands. On a whim, Gnik asked his new friend if he had a business card. "I just moved here, and I haven't met many people. If you don't mind, I'd like to stay connected."

The man rifled through his wallet and handed Gnik a card. He extended his hand again. "Steve. Steve Lawrence. Thanks again for helping me with my tire." Gnik apologized for not having a card to give in return. Making a mental note to get business cards, Gnik thanked Steve again for the ride to the library and promised to be in touch.

Later that evening when Gnik arrived home, he flipped on the television to have some background noise in the empty apartment. He turned on the computer and looked for comments on his morning blog post. He expected a reply from one of The Crew and was interested in their thoughts. The first comment popped up:

> Glad things are coming together, and I'm so glad you're finding joy in giving. I have found the same to be true. In fact, when I have some expectation of gaining something in return when I give, I end up being disappointed.

Gnik reflected on the observation from one of The Crew. He smiled, pleased that his friends were following his activities. He noticed that the second comment was from his dad. He eagerly read:

> There's something deeper in this lesson that you'll probably figure out soon, if you haven't already. It involves something you said about wanting to return the favor to Pam. Yes, you should give without any expectation of gaining anything in return. But, notice how you felt when Pam gave you her insight. You wanted to do something for her.
>
> When you give to others, it becomes easier for them to give to you.
>
> Give without expectation, and when the opportunity presents itself, receive with joy.
>
> Glad to know all's well with you.
>
> Dad

**When you give to others, it becomes easier for them to give to you. Give without expectation, and when the opportunity presents itself, receive with joy.**

Gnik's thoughts immediately turned to Steve and his flat tire. It truly was a joy for him to help Steve change the tire, but he hadn't realized at the time that Steve desired—and was almost compelled—to help him in return. He seemed very pleased when Gnik accepted his offer of a lift to the library.

Gnik made a commitment to himself that he would continue to help others without expecting anything in return. He realized that when we help each other, we all do better as a result.

# Gnik's Aha!

The Law of Reciprocity: What goes around comes around. If I help others, it is more likely that others will want to help me in return.

day **3**

# The Power of Perspective

Gnik rolled over and pulled the covers over his head, but not before he caught a glimpse of the gray sky outside. The curtains in his apartment moved slightly as the ceiling fan circulated the air. The sky was unusually dark, and his mood matched the weather.

Gnik finally pulled himself out of bed and took a long shower. As the warm water rained over his face, he deliberated about how to use the day. *I really should get out and meet some people. Make some contacts and see how I can help others.*

Ordinarily, he wouldn't need to convince himself to do something productive, but, today, he was feeling a bit out of sorts.

*On the other hand, I have some things that I really should take care of here at home. I have some organizing to do, and I'm just not feeling it today. I'll get my stuff together, and I'll be able to rock it tomorrow.*

Gnik wasn't comfortable detailing his "off" day on his public blog, so he took his funk to his Facebook wall, where only his close friends would see. Still, he decided to be subtle in his status update:

Today's a good day to sing the blues. :-/

While he felt justified in blowing the day off, he still felt conflicted. He knew he'd have days like this, but he hadn't expected one to show up so soon.

Hoping to clear his head, Gnik hastily threw on some warm-up pants and a T-shirt and finished getting ready to leave the house. He grabbed a banana and an apple, downed a glass of orange juice, and headed out toward the park. He loved people watching, and the nearby park seemed like a great place for it. Wrapped up in a dark cloud, Gnik slowly walked to a park bench near a footpath. He sat down, leaned back, stretched his legs out, and put his chin on his chest.

Gnik smiled faintly at the memory that had popped into his head when he entered the park. *"I was strolling through the park one night, and oh, I felt so blue ..."*

Gnik's parents used to sing these same words every time they took him to the park while he was growing up. The next line to the song "Little Space Girl" struck Gnik by how much it fit today. *"When I heard a little voice say, 'I'm so lonely, too.'"*

Gnik wondered to himself whether he might be lonely, when his thoughts were interrupted by someone saying his name. "Gnik? Gnik with a G?"

Gnik looked up, surprised that someone would recognize him after having been in town only a couple of days. "Hey, Gnik. Remember me? Pam. With a P."

Gnik stood up and took Pam's extended hand, shaking it weakly. "Hey, Pam. How's it going?"

"What was that, Gnik? That was one of the most pathetic handshakes ever!" Pam winked, but Gnik wasn't sure she was joking. He reached out and shook her hand again—a bit too vigorously this time.

"Sorry, Pam," he offered. "I'm having a rough day, so I came to the park to clear my head. Good to see you again, though. I have to thank you for your insight the other day—I really appreciate your helping me see that the gift is in the giving. I know it doesn't look like it, but that conversation stuck with me, and it's already made a difference."

Gnik looked up and finally made eye contact with Pam. The simple act of talking with her made him feel a little better about his day.

"Glad to be of service, Gnik. So, what's going on today? You're not the same guy I remember from the coffee shop. What's up?"

Gnik felt the sincerity in Pam's voice. As he explained his concerns, more frustrations and problems kept coming out. After a couple of minutes, he realized he was dousing Pam with a fire hose of complaints.

Pam listened patiently without reacting. Once Gnik finished pouring out his problems, she stepped back and looked him up and down. "So," she slowly began, "how long are you going to have a lousy day?"

"What?" Gnik was confused at the question. "How long? Just today, I guess. It's just a bad day. It'll be better tomorrow, I hope."

"Wow. That's a waste of the rest of the day."

When he didn't respond, Pam repeated her original question. "Let's try this again, Gnik. How long are you going to let today be lousy for you?"

"I don't understand what you're getting at. I woke up in a funk this morning. It's overcast and windy. The weather matches my mood perfectly, and tomorrow will be better."

"Gnik," Pam said, smiling, "you will find what you are looking for. For example, where you see a gloomy overcast day, I see a wonderfully cool, comfortable morning perfect for a walk in the park. The sun isn't too hot, and there's no glare to hurt my eyes—which is perfect, because I forgot my sunglasses."

## You will find what you are looking for.

Gnik was starting to catch on, but he wasn't convinced.

"Okay, but what about the fact that here I am, alone in a new city, and I have nothing?" Gnik was almost pleased with himself for contradicting Pam so easily.

"I'm jealous. You get to make a fresh start. No baggage holding you back. You can do—you can be—anything you want!"

Gnik had never considered that starting from scratch was a chance to reinvent himself. He caught himself smiling while he threw out a second complaint.

"What about the fact that I have no friends here?"

Pam feigned hurt feelings as she wiped away imaginary tears. "No friends? Well, you certainly couldn't actually meet *new* people, now, could you?"

He apologized and backpedaled. "You know what I mean. I left all my friends at home. I don't know anyone here. Except you, of course."

Pam looked into Gnik's eyes and made a direct hit.

"Gnik, you will find exactly what you are looking for. If you think today's a blah day, it will rise up and meet your blah expectations. On the other hand, if you look at today as your best day so far, it will be."

He sat in silence as Pam's message sunk in. "You're making it sound like I can change time and space," he joked.

"Actually, you're right. When you change how you look at something, the thing you're looking at changes. You can change time and space. So, let me ask you one more time. How long are you going to let today be lousy for you?"

"Ouch. I guess I'm done with the lousy day."

"Well, you don't sound very convinced," Pam lectured. "How long?" She threw a mock punch at Gnik's shoulder.

"It's not like a switch, Pam. I can't just turn on a great day."

"Gnik, it's exactly like a switch! Happiness brings success— not the other way around. Find things to be happy about rather than things to bring you down. It *is* a switch. Do you want it on or off? Decide, then do whatever you have to do to make it happen."

## Happiness brings success—not the other way around. Find things to be happy about rather than things to bring you down.

Pam looked at her watch. "It's been nice chatting, but I've got to run. Email me tonight and let me know how your day goes. For me, today's my best day ever, you know?"

Pam left Gnik immersed in his thoughts. He repositioned himself on the bench and looked out across the park's open field. He saw a young girl with her father holding a kite against the wind. Gnik smiled. *The wind is perfect today for kite flying. A perfect day for a man to spend with his daughter.* He smiled and left the park bench, intent on making today his best day ever.

# Gnik's Aha!

When I change how I look at something, then the thing I look at changes.

# day 4

# The Gift of Attention

The rain was coming down steadily. Gnik took a deep breath and looked out his apartment window. *The air smells so clean, and the grass is really looking green.* He laughed as he thought about Pam chastising him yesterday. *She was right about having a positive perspective. Look at all the people out there, hunched over and shuffling down the street. Rain is so cleansing. I wonder if they see it that way.*

Gnik grabbed an umbrella as he rushed out the door and hurried to the bus stop on the corner. It was time to head to the grocery store and pick up some sustenance. He could only stand to eat out for so long; he wanted a home-cooked meal, even if it was only his old college standby of macaroni and cheese. Most of the people he passed on the street didn't lift their eyes enough to notice his smile. As Gnik danced the final

steps into the covered shelter, he nodded to the line of passengers crowded inside, waiting for the bus.

"Mornin'! A little wet today, ain't it?" It seemed an elderly
man in a cap and trench coat wanted to start a conversation
with Gnik.

"I love the smell of the rain," Gnik said, grinning.

The man continued, "I guess it won't let up until afternoon.
I saw the weather report on Channel 4 this morning. I like
Channel 4 better than Channel 9. Their weather girl is right
most of the time. That guy on Channel 9 has been wrong
about the rainfall amounts the last three times! If I don't know
the weather and I forget my galoshes, my feet get wet and my
socks are soggy all day. I *hate* soggy socks."

Gnik's first instinct was to turn away and focus on his
smartphone, but he resisted the impulse. *This guy seems nice,
if a little odd. What have I got to lose by listening to him for a
few minutes?*

He turned to face the old man. "I know just what you
mean—I hate soggy socks myself."

The man saw his opening and barged through, developing
a complex conversation with little involvement from Gnik. An
occasional nod from Gnik was all that was necessary to keep
him going. Occasionally, Gnik caught his attention wandering
and quickly brought it back to the man with another nod, a
smile, and an "uh huh." Seven minutes later, the bus arrived.
As the passengers took their seats and Gnik lost sight of his
new friend, he found himself thinking that the interaction
had been quite enjoyable.

At the next stop, the old man passed Gnik on his way out. He placed a weathered hand on the younger man's shoulder. "Thanks for listening to me, young fella. Thank you very much."

Gnik was surprised at the depth of the old man's appreciation for such a simple gesture as listening. *That was so easy. I wonder...* He caught himself mid-thought. *I wonder what would happen if I spent my whole day listening, rather than talking.* He recalled a seldom-implemented adage from long ago suggesting that because we have two ears and one mouth, we should listen twice as much as we talk. *I'll try it,* he thought.

Lost in thought, Gnik was startled when the smartly dressed man sitting directly behind him leaned up and offered Gnik his hand.

"Good morning. I'm Garrett." Gnik awkwardly contorted his body to shake Garrett's hand. "I couldn't help but overhear your conversation with that gentleman."

Gnik smiled, as if they shared an inside secret. "He was certainly an entertaining conversation partner."

"Not only that," Garrett continued, "but when was the last time you were thanked for listening? Whatever you're doing, I think you're on to something important." Garrett stood up. "This is my stop, but I'd like to continue our conversation sometime and follow up on what I observed."

Garrett pulled a business card from his pocket and handed it to Gnik. "Have a great day, and thanks for listening." He winked and stepped off the bus.

During the rest of his bus ride, Gnik realized that people didn't do much talking, which made it hard for him to do much listening.

## We should listen twice as much as we talk.

At the grocery store, Gnik decided to try a new tactic. As he stood in the checkout line, he noticed the cashier's key ring had a baby photo on the fob. He pointed to it and said, "Cute baby." That was all it took. The cashier gushed during the entire transaction about how wonderful her baby was. She even offered advice, in case Gnik ever had kids of his own, on what brand of diapers are the best. Gnik smiled, nodded, and enjoyed the woman's enthusiasm for her child.

Gnik carried two bags of groceries in one hand and his umbrella and a third bag in the other as he walked back to the bus stop. As he found a seat on the bus, he noticed the guitar his seatmate was cradling. Remembering the commitment he'd made to himself that he would spend the day listening, he took a deep breath and asked, "Have you been playing long?"

The guitar player seemed to be about Gnik's age. His answer was brief. "About twelve years." He then realized that Gnik was intently focused on what he was saying. "I started when I was ten. Do you play?"

Gnik shook his head. "No. My mom made me take piano lessons, but I always wanted to learn the guitar."

The man spent the rest of the bus ride explaining to Gnik that it wasn't too late to take up the instrument, if he was still interested. As the bus approached Gnik's stop, he stood to disembark. "Thanks a lot for the advice," he said. "Maybe I'll take a lesson someday."

The guitar player reached into his pocket for a business card. "If you'd like to get started, I know some great instructors. Text me if you have any questions."

The two shook hands, and Gnik exited the bus. Though it was raining lightly, he decided the umbrella was more trouble than it was worth and dropped it into one of the grocery bags. He jogged to the end of the block and slipped into his building.

## Giving to others can be as simple as giving my time and attention.

As he put away the groceries, Gnik realized that a few minor changes in his approach to the trip had made a big impact on his experience. *Just listening and being friendly to that old guy sure made him feel good. The cashier loved talking about her baby, and now I know someone who can teach me guitar. And all I had to do was listen.* His thoughts flashed back to his dad's comment, *When you give to others, it becomes easier for them to give to you.*

"I had no idea that just listening could have that effect," he said aloud, and then it hit him: *Giving to others can be as simple as giving my time and attention.*

Gnik looked out the window. It was late afternoon, and the sun was beginning to peek through the clouds. The rain had let up, and the colors of the sunset were beginning to show. *What a day. I can hardly wait to see what tomorrow brings!* He sat at his corner desk and typed a quick blog update:

> It's amazing how small gestures can generate big results. Listening—*really* listening—is a seemingly small and insignificant act, but the payoff can be huge!

# Gnik's Aha!

I can give others the gift of my attention. I should listen twice as much as I speak. When I speak, I learn what I know. When I listen, I learn what others know.

# 5

# It's All About Them

The beeping of the alarm on Gnik's smartphone grew louder, but he had already been awake for nearly half an hour, as thoughts about how powerful listening could be bounced around his head. He grew more and more excited about the lessons he had learned yesterday. As he absentmindedly reached for his phone and silenced the alarm, he decided to call his college debate partner, Kelli, and share his recent experiences.

Gnik and Kelli had been a very successful debate team. The two had often developed strategies that had led to their success in competitions. Of course, listening to the arguments of the other side was paramount, but Gnik had never considered the power that listening might have in his everyday life.

Listening can instantly transform a conversation. If anyone would appreciate his new insight, Gnik thought, it was Kelli.

## Listening can instantly transform a conversation.

Gnik took his time eating breakfast to make sure that when he called, Kelli would be awake and ready to talk. His thoughts turned to yesterday's bus ride, the old man, and the cashier at the grocery store, as he relived the high points of his day.

The single beep from Gnik's watch signaled that it was now 10 o'clock. He picked up the phone to dial Kelli. After three rings, she answered.

"Gnik! It's so good to hear from you!" she said excitedly. "I've been thinking about you—how are you doing?"

"I've been good. I was—"

"That's great, Gnik," Kelli interrupted. "Where are you living now?"

Gnik described his recent move from home, the city where he now lived, and his new experiences. He sensed, though, that Kelli wasn't entirely focused on what he was saying. He stopped talking for a moment and asked, "What about you? How have you been?"

Kelli gushed, "I'm engaged!"

"Wow! That's great. Tell me about him."

Gnik suddenly remembered the importance of listening, and, though he still wanted to share his insight from yesterday, he realized that applying the listening principle was more important now than sharing his theory. He listened as Kelli described her fiancé and how they met. She continued with the story of how he proposed, and, when she described the setting of their ideal wedding, Gnik found himself completely engaged in the vivid description of the ceremony that would take place later that year. She wanted Gnik at the wedding, of course.

"He sounds like a great guy, Kelli, and you know I wouldn't miss your wedding for the world."

After Kelli finished describing her wedding plans, Gnik found an opportunity to change the subject. He was eager to share his recent epiphany with his friend.

"Kelli, remember when we were on the debate team and how we'd strategize? There was that one time that we were comparing ideas before the finals and—"

"Hey, before I forget," Kelli interrupted, "I was talking to my brother, Chris, the other day, and he told me something that immediately made me think of you. What are you doing these days?"

"I'm hoping to start my own marketing business, Kelli, but I—"

"This will be perfect for you, Gnik! He told me about a question that has gotten some major traction for him in his business."

Gnik's frustration at being constantly interrupted immediately evaporated. He thought, *I have to know more about this question.* He noticed that Kelli had paused slightly. "I'm all ears, Kelli. Tell me more."

Kelli's enthusiasm was contagious. She explained, "Chris has been reading this book about building better business relationships, and one of the things he's learned is to ask your potential client, 'What's something—not related to your business—that you feel passionate about?'"

Gnik was confused. "Why doesn't he try to help with something related to their work?"

"Because," Kelli explained, "he wants to find something they're *passionate* about—that's really the key. Since he started asking this question, the results have been phenomenal. First, he's developing an understanding of his clients and their *personal* passions, rather than just their attitudes toward business. Later, when he comes across someone who has the skills or connections to help with the client's passionate project, he looks like a hero when he connects the two."

Kelli continued. "For example, Chris has a client who handles commercial real estate properties. During a conversation, Chris asked his client what invigorates him, what makes him feel alive. His client immediately answered, 'Music.' As they kept talking, Chris learned that his real estate client is an accomplished drummer. He connected his client with a friend who plays the electric guitar. Since then, the two have gotten together several times just to jam. In fact, Chris says that both of them still thank him for putting them in contact with each other."

Gnik's excitement grew as he considered the possibilities.

Gnik finally looked at his watch and realized they had been on the phone for nearly two hours. Wanting to be respectful of his friend's time and schedule, he thanked her for the advice and congratulated her again on the big news. When they'd hung up, he leaned back in his chair, thinking about how connecting with people's passions might play out in his own business and relationships. Then it hit him that the entire purpose of his call was to talk about listening, but he'd never had a chance to bring it up. Yet, in spite of that, he felt he'd gained so much from the conversation.

Gnik replayed the conversation with Kelli in his head. He thought of how frustrated he had been at first, when she seemed uninterested in what he had to say. *But she wasn't uninterested*, he realized. *She was just so excited about what she wanted to say that she couldn't listen to what I had to say. Kelli wasn't trying to be rude. What she had to say was more important than what I had to say.* Gnik realized the importance may have been relative, but he also recognized that he gained a far greater benefit from having listened to Kelli today than he would have from simply relating his own observations on listening.

*That makes a lot of sense*, he concluded. *If what a person has to say is more important than what I have to say, then it's even more important for me to listen.*

Gnik pondered Kelli's question and realized he didn't know most of his acquaintances well enough to understand what they were passionate about. He hadn't thought much about his own passions lately, either. His status update, he hoped, would cause some of them to think about—and maybe to share—what they were excited about:

What is something—not related to your business—that energizes you?

Gnik clicked the Publish button and closed the cover of his laptop. He sat back, thinking about what energized him.

# Gnik's Aha!

 What the other person has to say is more important than what I have to say.

# day 6

# Link Up and Connect

The sunlight started to peek through a crack in the curtains, and Gnik stirred as he began to wake. He lay just far enough from the rogue sunbeam to notice the brightness without being blinded by it. He closed his eyes and replayed the highlights of the past few days. *Listening*, he reminded himself. *I still can't believe how powerful a little listening can be.*

Gnik's mind flashed back to Garrett and the man on the bus. Instinctively, he reached for his growing stack of business cards from the past few days. Flipping through them, he found Garrett's. As he looked at the raised lettering on the card, he noticed for the first time a printed invitation to "Connect with me on LinkedIn," followed by a website address. Garrett's Facebook and Twitter information were also printed on the card. Gnik leaned back in his bed, holding the card in front of his eyes. He read the details on the card again, and his smile grew with a new realization.

*Online social networks can be used for more than keeping up with friends. I can leverage Facebook, LinkedIn, Twitter, and even my blog to increase my ability to connect with people.* Gnik knew the basics of online networking, and this new understanding of using his social networks to further his personal networks was energizing. He felt the urgency of getting his online presence set.

## Online social networks can be used for more than keeping up with friends.

Gnik debated the pros and cons of sitting in his apartment or going out somewhere public to do his online work. The tools were available either way, but he decided that leaving the apartment would provide additional benefits. First, he liked the idea of going somewhere—simply having a destination increased his focus. Second, he wanted to be open to meet someone whom he could help or who could help him. He gathered his laptop and a pad of paper, shut the apartment building door behind him, and walked down the street to the coffee shop.

Gnik found a table, settled in, and jumped online. He'd been thinking his name could be a great web address, and, when a domain name search showed that gnikrowten.com was available, he purchased it. He would put the website together later;

for now, he was just happy to have staked a claim on his own corner of the internet. Eventually, he would move his blog to gnikrowten.com.

Next, Gnik decided to focus on the social networks. He had previously started setting up his LinkedIn account but had never finished. Remembering Garrett's business card, Gnik thought, *If I'm going to connect with Garrett on LinkedIn, I need to be on LinkedIn.* As he completed his profile, he realized he could begin to brand himself as a marketing consultant right from the start. He put his new job title in his updated profile, then he sat back to examine his handiwork. He felt like he was making progress, and he was beginning to feel like his business idea was becoming a reality.

*Two down, two to go,* Gnik thought. He knew there were dozens of social networking options, but he wanted to focus his energies on the most widely used programs. He turned his attention to Twitter. Gnik wasn't very familiar with the microblogging site, but he wasn't going to let that keep him from claiming his name. Today, his focus was getting his accounts set up, rather than connecting with all of his contacts. *Connecting will come later. If I don't at least get started, it will be too easy to keep procrastinating.* He was pleased that he was able to use his name for his handle and made a mental note: *I need to put @GnikRowten on my business card.*

## If I don't at least get started, it will be too easy to keep procrastinating.

37

Finally, Gnik pulled up his Facebook account. He had already set up his profile so that people could find him at facebook.com/GnikRowten, and for a moment he let his mind wander as his eyes glazed over the activity on his wall. He knew it was important to have an online presence, and he knew there were different ways he could approach his online marketing, but he wasn't sure what would work best for him. He closed the cover of his laptop, pushed it away, and slid the notepad in its place. He found a clean sheet of paper and sketched a chart with four columns labeled *Blog, Facebook, Twitter,* and *LinkedIn.* On one side of the chart, Gnik wrote a few questions: *Why should I use this method? How will I use it? Who will I connect with?* and *What marketing opportunities exist?* He left a couple of blank rows that he could fill in with other questions he might think of later.

| | Blog | Facebook | Twitter | LinkedIn |
|---|---|---|---|---|
| Why should I use this method? | | | | |
| How will I use it? | | | | |
| Who will I connect with? | | | | |
| What marketing opportunities exist? | | | | |
| | | | | |
| | | | | |

As he tapped the point of his pencil in one of the empty boxes, he thought about the different purposes of the various online tools he'd set up. *Different, but complementary*, he thought. He visualized his online presence as information content supported by a set of networking tools he could use to brand and promote his business. He would provide information through his online presence. He could then use his online networking tools to cross-market and to brand and promote his business.

Gnik stretched his legs out under the table and clasped his hands behind his head. He closed his eyes to think more deeply about some of his self-imposed questions. *How can I make all these tools work together?* He opened his eyes and saw a poster on the coffee shop wall. At the bottom, he noticed the familiar phrase, "Visit our website ..." Thinking of it as research, he opened his laptop and typed the web address. Scanning the information on the webpage, he began to laugh when he saw the phrase at the bottom of the page, "Friend us on Facebook."

*Of course!* Gnik thought. *I can use Facebook to send people to my blog, and I can invite my blog readers to follow me on Twitter.* He smiled as he jotted a few notes into his chart, indicating that he wanted to encourage his friends to connect with him on other social platforms.

After filling in a few more boxes on his chart, Gnik turned back to his laptop and wrote a new blog post:

> Listen. Whatever you're doing right now, stop. And listen.
>
> What do you hear now that you weren't hearing before? I'm writing this from a noisy coffee shop. I just noticed dishes clinking in the back, and I can

hear the hiss of the steam machine. I hear bits and pieces of conversations, and the dull hum of traffic outside.

My challenge to you is to try this exercise again during your next conversation. Stop, and really listen. Don't entertain your own thoughts of how you plan to respond to what you are hearing. Listen. Really listen. I promise you'll have a wonderful experience.

And please follow me on Twitter@GnikRowten.

Gnik inserted a link to his Twitter page and posted the new entry. He went to his Facebook page and updated his status to include a link to his new blog post:

Check the blog for my latest lesson learned.

He wouldn't include a link to another social media outlet in *every* new post, but it was a start, and he was pleased with himself for taking quick action.

# Gnik's Aha!

I can leverage online social networks to increase opportunities to connect with others.

day

**7**

# Ask the Right Questions

The phone rang while Gnik was in that sleepy-and-not-quite-awake stage, startling him with the unexpected sound. He decided to let the call go to voicemail while he gathered his thoughts and put some plans together for the day. He still felt a little off-balance in this new town, as the last few days had been a whirlwind of new experiences for him.

*Well*, Gnik thought, *I might as well keep the whirlwind moving.* He found Garrett's business card again, and he dialed the number. Not knowing what to say or even if the man would remember their short encounter, Gnik pressed Send on his phone. After two rings, a gentle voice answered.

"Garrett here."

"Hi, Garrett," Gnik began. "I don't know if you remember me, but we chatted on the bus the other day. This is Gnik. Gnik Rowten."

"Of course, Gnik. I'm so glad you called. If you have some time, I'd like to meet with you. What do you think?"

Gnik was nervous, not knowing what to expect, but he agreed. "Sure. I'd like to meet."

"Great!" Garrett replied enthusiastically. "Why don't you come to my office around lunchtime, and we'll grab a bite and talk?" They confirmed the details and ended the call.

A few hours later, Gnik was brimming with anticipation as he entered an impressive-looking office building. He gave his name to the lobby security guard, who called Garrett's office to announce his arrival. The guard hung up and turned to Gnik. "He's on his way down."

Gnik rested in an overstuffed leather chair at the edge of the lobby. A few minutes later, Garrett emerged from the elevator and greeted him with a smile and handshake. The men walked together down the hallway on the opposite side of the lobby, through a heavy set of doors that opened into the building's cafeteria. Garrett grabbed a tuna melt, and Gnik got an Asian chicken wrap. They found a table outside in the warm sun.

Gnik started. "When we met on the bus, you said you wanted to follow up with me on what you'd observed. I'm curious about that."

Garrett smiled and finished chewing his bite of tuna sandwich. "Let me start with a couple of questions. Tell me a little about yourself, Gnik. Where are you from, and what do you do?"

Gnik took a sip of his soda. "Well, I moved here about a week ago, and I'm trying to get started as a marketing consultant. I don't really have any business prospects yet, but I'm not letting it get me down. I know it can take some time to make the right connections."

"The guy on the bus," Garrett said. "What was that all about?"

Gnik wasn't sure how to answer at first but decided to be blunt. "I guess you could call it an experiment—an experiment in listening. Once he started talking, I was curious to see how it might play out. So I listened, and it turned out to be the start of a really good day."

Garrett nodded, encouraging Gnik to continue.

"In fact, I've had a tremendous week. I've learned some great lessons, but I'm missing something. I want to make useful business connections, but I haven't done any aggressive networking yet. I'm hoping to learn how to make my contacts with people more beneficial—more *mutually* beneficial."

Garrett paused and took a breath. "Tell me, Gnik, why do you want to start your own business?"

The question was a new one for Gnik. He reflected a moment before saying he was interested in freedom and flexibility.

"Next question," Garrett continued. "Why hasn't networking worked for you in the past?"

For a moment, Gnik thought Garrett was kidding, but there was no evidence of it on his face. "Well, networking is kind of awkward. People shoving business cards at each other. It seems so hit-or-miss."

"Last question." Garrett paused. "What is the purpose of asking questions?"

"Well," Gnik began, "I can find out if someone needs my marketing services, for example. Questions are a useful way to gather information."

Garrett adjusted his position in his seat. He looked at Gnik as if he had something important to say. "True. You can always use a question to gather information. Teachers do that, right? *Did you complete the assignment, Gnik?* They're just getting information. But think about the larger role of questions. If you ask the *right* questions, you get people to think. When they think, they get energized. When they are energized, they become more connected with you. The better the question, the better the connection."

He continued, "When you ask great questions, you affirm a person's value in your relationship. When you affirm their value to you, your connection with them—and their connection with you—is strengthened. The bottom line is, asking great questions will always get you farther than looking for the right answers."

Gnik was stunned. He hadn't thought of it like this before, but he had been looking for answers. He'd had some positive listening experiences, but he'd been looking for some sort of answer by practicing his listening. Now, if he could figure out the art of asking great questions ... the prospects were exciting!

# If you ask the *right* questions, you get people to think. When they think, they get energized. When they are energized, they become more connected with you. The better the question, the better the connection.

"I see what you mean, Garrett," he said, "but how can I learn to ask great questions?"

Garrett laughed. "That's the challenge. Here are a few ideas. Think about why you're asking the question. Questions are powerful. For example, if your girlfriend asks, 'You're not going out wearing *that*, are you?,' is she really asking you if you're going to wear that outfit?"

"No," Gnik said, laughing at the mental image of the clothing choices that would prompt that question.

"Make sure the questions you ask affirm the value of the relationship. For example, think about the first questions I asked you, about who you are and what you do. Did that affect how you viewed me or our conversation?"

"It sure did," Gnik said. "I thought, this guy must really be interested in me for some reason."

"Exactly! Make sure the questions you ask affirm the value of the other person in your relationship. To your other point— about networking being hit-or-miss? What if you changed the way you thought of it?"

Gnik looked up, unsure of what Garrett meant. "I don't understand."

"What if you just went out, met people, and enjoyed the interactions. Would that seem awkward and hit-or-miss?"

"Of course not," Gnik said immediately.

# Questions are powerful.

"Excellent. Then that's what networking should be for you. The other stuff will follow. Let's talk about that in more detail some time. It's been a great lunch, but I have an appointment back in my office in a few minutes. Would you like to meet again next week?"

Gnik nodded enthusiastically. "Next week is great—but can I ask you one more question before you leave?"

Garrett smiled his approval.

"Is it really that useful to connect with people on LinkedIn?"

"Great question. We'll talk more about that next time we meet, but the short answer is that I've decided I can't have too many friends! Meantime, I hope you'll connect with me on LinkedIn, Gnik."

Gnik smiled. "Thanks for your time, Garrett. I learned a lot."

The two men stood and shook hands. As Garrett started to walk away, he turned back and called out to Gnik. "Keep working on your questions!"

Gnik gathered the leftovers from lunch and threw the trash away. He refilled his soda and walked home. Musing on the lunchtime conversation with Garrett, he started thinking of questions he could ask people that would affirm their value. It was easier than he thought when he focused on it.

*"Tell me about your family."*

*"How did you get involved in that industry?"*

*"Why did you start your own business?"*

Just then he flashed back to Kelli's question from the other day: "What's something—not related to your business—that you feel passionate about?" *That's a great question,* Gnik realized. Remembering his Facebook update asking that very question, he opened his laptop to see if any of his friends had responded. When he pulled up the page, he was surprised at the number and variety of people who'd commented. He took a few minutes to read through the comments. Some of the answers were quite personal, and he felt privileged to have been granted access into the deep centers of his friends' lives.

*Questions* are *powerful,* Gnik realized. *Asking the right questions can totally change the way I've been networking.*

# Gnik's Aha!

Great questions affirm the other person's value. Rather than focus on questions that recall knowledge, I should ask questions that affirm value.

day 8

# The Value of
# What *They* Know

Starting the day by surfing the web wasn't the norm for Gnik. Instinctively, he knew there had to be better things to do with his time, but he decided to indulge, for a few minutes anyway, in catching up on overnight news and sports scores. He decided he might as well check his email, too, and scanned the influx of mail that had hit his inbox while he was asleep. He deleted the spam and a couple of emails that he had no interest in reading. One subject line, however, caught his attention: "Pam (with a P) has sent you an invitation." While he assumed the message had been generated by some automated service or another, Pam's personalized subject line encouraged him to open it immediately:

Gnik, I'm in Orlando at a conference, and I just got word that the speaker here will be doing a presentation back home in a couple of months. I've had a tremendous experience, and I've learned a lot. I thought you might benefit by attending the local seminar. Click on the link below for details.

The content of the email surprised Gnik. He had a great deal of respect for Pam, and he was surprised to learn she was one of those "seminar people." Growing up, he had seen the big names come through town—Zig Ziglar, Tony Robbins, and Les Brown, among others. He had borrowed some of their presentations on CD or DVD from the library, but the content didn't seem to be all that earth-shattering. In fact, most of it struck him as just plain common sense. So, he had decided long ago not to waste his time or money attending seminars. He sent Pam a quick email response, explaining that he wasn't much of a "seminar person" and wasn't sure he'd be able to make it to this one.

However, even as he clicked the Send button, Gnik found that Pam's message had shaken his anti-seminar mindset. Was it possible he'd been missing the point all these years?

He completed his morning routine and walked out of his apartment. As the bright sunlight hit him in the face, he squinted to keep it out of his eyes. He'd need to buy a pair of sunglasses eventually, and today would be as good a day as any.

Inside the drugstore, Gnik noticed that the man in line ahead of him was carrying a book by one of the motivational experts he had previously regarded with skepticism. The coincidence piqued his curiosity about the author. He tapped the man on the shoulder. "Is that book any good?"

The man turned and smiled kindly. He held up the book and nodded. "I've read all of his books—this is one of my favorites. It's phenomenal."

Gnik decided not to confess his lack of passion for the author and simply said, "It looks interesting." He suddenly recognized an opportunity to ask some great questions. "What impact has the book had on you?"

The man excused himself for a moment so that he could complete his transaction at the register. He paused while Gnik paid for his sunglasses. The two stepped off to the side and out of the way of other store patrons. "Good question. One thing it has helped me realize is that we're all pretty much the same."

Gnik caught himself thinking that he might have been right all along to be suspicious of these books, discs, and seminars. Even so, he asked the man, who introduced himself as Russell, to explain.

"Well, for a lot of years, I lived a pretty mediocre life. I was coasting. I didn't push myself to do anything, and I got mediocre results. I saw others with phenomenal lives, and I assumed it was because they had phenomenal talent or phenomenal luck. Then I read this book. I realized that this guy isn't any smarter than I am, nor is he any luckier than I am. He gets afraid to step outside of his comfort zone, just like I do. He has low days, just like I do. The biggest difference is that he ignored those things, and he went after his goals. This book, for example, tells the story of how he made his first million."

**This guy isn't any smarter than I am, nor is he any luckier than I am. He gets afraid to step outside of his comfort zone, just like I do. He has low days, just like I do. The biggest difference is that he ignored those things.**

Gnik was intrigued and found his mind suddenly open to the possibilities. After thanking Russell for his time, he decided to make a stop at the library. There, he selected a book and CD series that looked interesting. He read the first few pages of the book and found they grabbed him. After checking out, he put the book and CD set into his backpack and headed back to his apartment.

At home, Gnik turned on his laptop and pulled up his email. He absentmindedly scanned the incoming email and noticed a response from Pam. He was embarrassed by the email he'd sent earlier today and instantly wished he could unsend it, but was interested in Pam's response:

> Gnik, a lot of people I know aren't "seminar people," but I have to tell you that I've met some of the most successful people I know networking at seminars. This one has been amazing! I hope you'll consider attending when it comes to town. It's one of the best ways that I have found to keep learning and growing. One seminar speaker I've seen, Charlie "Tremendous" Jones, said that we'll be the same five years from now as we are now, except for the books we've read and the people we've met. In that

statement, I include the seminars I attend and any related material I read and listen to.

Gnik immediately registered for the seminar. Then he closed his laptop and began reading the book he'd just brought home. He had a notepad nearby, and he jotted down a few notes as he read.

# Gnik's Aha!

I need to constantly feed my mind and my network. There is no substitute for facts, information, knowledge, and connections.

day

# Stand Up and Stand Out

Waking early, Gnik was on his way to the local office supply store by nine. He knew it was silly to feel excited about shopping for business cards, but it was the first time in his life he'd have a card with his own company name on it. He had worked out all the contact details and created a colorful logo. At the store, he took his time flipping through pages of sample cards. He savored the feel of the different card stocks and considered the various color and ink options. He wanted a card that would represent him well, but nothing flashy.

As he made his choices and placed a conservative initial order, Gnik envisioned himself proudly handing cards out to his contacts. A few hours later, the cards were ready for pickup, and he returned to the store. Pulling out a small stack of the perfectly cut cards, he fanned them out as if he were a magician performing sleight of hand. The design that the spread-out cards made was unique and, in a way, pleasing to look at. Gnik stared at it for a few moments.

He squared the cards and put the stack in his shirt pocket. He pulled out his phone and scrolled through yesterday's emails to find the details of the networking meeting he had registered for last night. While searching for networking groups, he found one that had an event scheduled for today. He made a note of the address.

Although he'd only been here a little over a week, Gnik was beginning to feel quite at home in the city and appreciative of its unique personality. He walked down the congested street with confidence, in spite of not knowing the exact location of his meeting. *If I get lost, I can always ask someone for directions*, he thought, smiling, *and that chance meeting might even turn into something bigger.*

Gnik arrived at the meeting place and made a name tag for himself. The "G" on his tag was prominent, and he expected that the unusual spelling of his name would be a useful conversation starter here, as it had been at similar gatherings. He found an agenda for the meeting and entered the room, looking around as if searching for someone he knew. He quickly realized how unlikely it was that he'd recognize anyone and instead began looking for someone who wasn't already deep in conversation. He glanced at his watch and saw he had about 12 minutes of networking time before the program started. He saw someone struggling to pour a drink at the refreshment table while also holding a notepad.

He walked over, stood next to the young man, and poured two sodas.

"Here," Gnik offered, and the man thanked him as he reached for one of the cups. He shoved the notepad under his arm and moved his drink to his left hand, offering to shake Gnik's hand.

"Thanks. I'm Israel. My friends call me Izzy." Izzy looked at Gnik's name tag and smiled. "Ga-Nick? Am I saying that right?"

"It's Gnik, with a G. Nice to meet you, Izzy." Gnik remembered his conversation with Garrett a few days ago and remembered that asking good questions to affirm other people's value is far more productive than searching for the perfect business contact.

"I'm new in town, Izzy. Tell me a little about yourself."

Izzy gave Gnik a standard 30-second commercial about the importance of life insurance. He asked Gnik if he knew anyone who needed more coverage. Gnik answered by asking Izzy another question: "What got you interested in life insurance?"

The insurance salesman stopped for a second, squaring his shoulders. Looking directly into Gnik's eyes, he told a poignant story about a close friend whose family struggled because a loved one died without coverage.

**Asking good questions to affirm other people's value is far more productive than searching for the perfect business contact.**

"I can't stand the thought of anyone else going through that. I want to help people protect themselves."

Gnik felt the sincerity of Izzy's passion, and he gave Izzy his card. "The program is starting in a few minutes. If you don't mind, though, I'd like to continue our conversation later."

Izzy accepted the card and examined it. He looked at both sides and, as he handed Gnik his own card, asked, "You do marketing consulting? I can use some help with my marketing. Do you have a LinkedIn or Facebook group where people can share ideas?"

Before Gnik could answer, the session was called to order. Gnik and Izzy found seats next to each other. Gnik wrote himself a note to learn about LinkedIn and Facebook groups.

The speaker, a celebrity in his industry, began his presentation by holding up the front page of the morning paper, which included a prominent photo of him. Gnik had never heard of the man but was impressed with his credentials: author, newspaper columnist, and frequent radio and TV talk show guest. Gnik listened closely as the speaker said, "How will people know you exist unless they see you? Unless they meet you? The secret is to get noticed and be remembered. You have to be seen to be successful."

Gnik's thoughts swirled around the idea of being noticed. He didn't think of himself as particularly shy, but he'd never sought the spotlight. *How will people know I exist unless they see me?* The question rolled around his head, as he thought about what it would take to get noticed.

The speaker finally closed by saying, "I'm no different from you—I just put myself in situations where I'm sure to be noticed."

Gnik was puzzled. *How can he say he's no different from me? He's well-known, and I'm completely unknown.* Then a thought popped into his head: *I wonder how hard it would be to become known as a specialist within my industry?* He had been reading up on a number of innovative marketing techniques firms could use to increase their business locally, and it was an area where he felt he could excel. In order to become known as the go-to guy for this marketing specialty, he'd first have to step outside his comfort zone and let the spotlight shine on him.

### How will people know you exist unless they see you? Unless they meet you? The secret is to get noticed and be remembered. You have to be seen to be successful.

At that moment, it hit Gnik that he should brand himself not as just another marketing consultant, but as a local expert. He would find new opportunities to connect with people during established networking events and at events he would create himself, and begin to be known as an expert.

After the meeting ended, Gnik hurried home, eager to start outlining his new plan. He found several informative articles about setting up networking groups, including groups on

LinkedIn and Facebook. He pulled up his social media profiles and began setting up his own local groups.

# Gnik's Aha!

The bottom line of networking is being visible. I must be seen, heard, and noticed in order to have the success I desire.

day **10**

# Who Do They Know?

The day started early for Gnik, since he wanted to get out and meet some business owners. If he was going to be visible, he needed to go where his potential clients were—whether that was a networking event, a chamber meeting, or even individual places of business. He thought about Pam as he walked to the coffee shop, where he would plan his day. He had come to think of Pam as a mentor, informal as the relationship was, and he knew he'd gain insight and direction by talking with her about his latest ideas. He hoped she'd be there.

Arriving at the coffee shop, Gnik decided to try something new. He asked for a shot of caramel in his beverage and dropped a generous tip in the jar for the barista. He turned to where he and Pam had sat the day they met, but the chairs were empty. He claimed a small area, then spread out his notepad and a couple of books. He pulled out a pen and began listing his priorities for the day.

Deep in thought, Gnik was slightly startled when he heard his name. "Gnik?" Pam was standing behind him, her coffee in one hand and her iPad in the other. "Is this seat taken, or can I squeeze in?"

"Good to see you again, Pam," Gnik said, as he squared up the books that were strewn across the table and made room for her. "I was wondering if I'd run into you today."

"Yeah, we just got a wedding, so I'm here to start putting things together."

Pam's phrasing struck Gnik as a little unusual. He didn't know what her business was, but by her comment, he assumed she was a wedding planner. "That's great, Pam, but what do you mean, you got a wedding?"

She smiled. "Ah, I see there's more for us to talk about." She repositioned herself in her seat, shifting her attention from her notes and iPad to focus completely on Gnik.

"So, excellent question, Gnik," she said. "Are you ready for the answer?"

Sensing that this conversation might provide some unexpected insights, Gnik grabbed a pen and opened his notebook. He wanted to be prepared for what she was about to say, yes, but it had also occurred to him that taking notes might curb his tendency to be distracted by his own agenda.

"I'm ready." He looked up in anticipation.

"Are you on LinkedIn?"

The question seemed bizarre, and Gnik couldn't figure out what it had to do with getting a wedding. He nodded, "I set up a LinkedIn account the other day, but I don't have any connections yet."

"Okay, let's start with another question. Do you know what my business is? I'll buy you coffee next time if you're right."

Gnik smiled smugly. He was pretty confident that his powers of observation had just earned him a free coffee. He paused for a moment, mostly for effect. "You're a wedding planner, aren't you, Pam?"

She chuckled and shook her head. "Nice try, but no. Want to guess again? If you're wrong a second time, of course, *you're* buying."

Gnik nodded his agreement as he thought hard, trying to put together the few pieces of information he had on Pam. It was something wedding-related ... something that gave her flexibility in when and where she worked ... something that would give her a reason to attend that conference the other day.

"Well," he stalled. He didn't have a clue, so he took a wild guess. "Are you a pastor?"

Pam laughed. "You owe me a coffee, Gnik! I own a limousine service."

"A limo service? I never would have guessed. So, when you say 'We got a wedding ...'"

"Let me ask you a question, Gnik. Have you ever gotten sick?" Her question seemed random, and Gnik had yet to find any nuggets of wisdom to write on his pad.

He put his pen down and looked at her, confused. "Sure I've been sick, but what does that have to do with anything?"

She proceeded. "Tell me about the last time you had to go to the doctor or the dentist—a time when they weren't able to help you themselves."

Gnik leaned back in his chair. "I'm not sure if this is what you're looking for, but a couple of months ago I was playing a pick-up game of basketball. After taking a shot, I felt something pop in my shoulder. It was painful when I touched it, so I went to my doctor the next day. He referred me to an orthopedic specialist, who treated me, then sent me for physical therapy. My shoulder's good as ever now. Is that what you mean?"

"That's exactly what I mean," Pam said, nodding. "Why didn't you go see the orthopedic doctor in the first place?"

"Well, for starters, I had no idea he was the person I needed to talk to. Besides, I doubt my insurance would have paid for a trip to a specialist without a referral from my own doctor."

Pam's expression changed to a knowing smile. "Interesting. I'm fascinated that so many people understand this basic concept of business networking, but they fail to implement it in their own businesses." She paused for a moment, letting her words sink in.

"So, Gnik, my question for you is, who is your doctor?"

Gnik felt like he was missing the point. "I don't have one here yet," he said.

"No, Gnik. Think of yourself as the orthopedic specialist. Who is the doctor in *your* business who refers business to you?"

A light bulb went on in Gnik's brain; he wrote Pam's question in his notebook. He stared at the question for at least a minute before she continued.

"Gnik, in my limo service, I handle clients ranging from celebrities visiting the city to birthday parties and proms to weddings and honeymoons. I've found that if someone calls me to hire a limo for a wedding, for example, they usually have other wedding-related needs."

Gnik nodded, beginning to see how things were coming together.

"I have a friend who's a photographer and another who is a wedding planner. I have a friend who makes cakes and another who does floral design. Not too long ago, I met someone who owns a banquet hall, and I even know a great caterer. We have found that many times, if one of us gets a wedding, we *all* get it."

Gnik smiled, then closed his eyes for a few seconds to focus on the possibilities that were suddenly bouncing around in his head. Then he looked at Pam.

"When someone calls for a limo," she said, "I ask if they need flowers or a caterer or a photographer. We've created our own wedding network, so we all get a share of the business. Obviously, I get business from the network that I didn't find myself.

"I know you're just starting your business, Gnik," she continued, "but setting up this type of network for yourself is very powerful. I'm going to give you a jump-start technique you can begin using today to expand your business network exponentially."

Gnik put the point of his pen on the next line of his paper. He would love to see his business explode.

"The eight magic words of networking. Are you ready?"

Gnik nodded. He wiped his hands on his pants and repositioned his pen.

Slowly, Pam said, "I ... know ... someone ... who ... can ... get ... that ... done."

Gnik wrote the words down and read them aloud. "I know someone who can get that done." He looked at her, suddenly remembering her opening question. "I understand how that works for your weddings, Pam, but I don't see what it has to do with me being on LinkedIn."

"You haven't really used it yet then, have you? The whole point of LinkedIn is to help business contacts connect with each other. Once you're in, you can find business professionals who are connected with the people you want to connect with."

He was still puzzled. "I just moved here, Pam, and I don't have any LinkedIn connections. So, the reality is, I *don't* know someone who can get that done."

## I know someone who can get that done.

"But you know *me*," she said, "and if you connect with me on LinkedIn, you'll find out soon enough that your network isn't just the people you know. It includes all the people and talent you can gain access to. So, when you meet someone who needs something, just say, 'I know someone who can get that done.' If you don't actually know someone, come see me, and together we'll figure it out. You'll end up being the hero, and everybody wins."

## Your network isn't just the people you know. It includes all the people and talent you can gain access to.

"I know someone who can get that done," Gnik repeated. "That's powerful. I like it!"

"I promise it will pay off for you, Gnik. Let's get together again soon—I want to hear how it's going. Besides," she said with a wink, "you owe me a coffee!"

"I know someone who can get *that* done," Gnik said with a grin as he handed Pam his newly minted business card. They shook hands as official members of each other's network.

# Gnik's Aha!

 My network isn't only people I know or who know me. It includes all the people and talent I have access to.

# 11

# It's Not Personal

Gnik woke up with an uncomfortable realization: *If I'm going to be serious about developing my business, it's time to get serious about developing my network.* The weight of this realization grew heavier on his mind. He shut his eyes tight against the bright morning sun and pulled the covers over his head. Then, a fear of the unknown began to surface.

*"Don't mind Gnik, he's just shy,"* Gnik thought, recalling his mother's words as he thought about how uncomfortable he felt reaching out and making contact with people he didn't know. *"He's just shy. He's just shy."*

Thinking about it, he grew angry—though not with his mother. She'd done the best she could in describing his quiet demeanor. No, he was angry with himself for letting these words she'd spoken more than a dozen years ago continue to affect how he thought of himself. *I don't think of myself as being shy*, Gnik thought. *Shy is timid. Shy is being easily frightened. No, I'm not shy.* He repeated the words to himself. *I'm not shy!*

## If I'm going to be serious about developing my business, it's time to get serious about developing my network.

Gnik decided the best antidote for the gloomy mood that was beginning to grip him was to hop out of bed and ready himself for the day's adventures. He turned on his internet radio, showered, shaved, dressed, and ate his breakfast in a rush. He realized he didn't know why he was in such a hurry, but the sense of urgency seemed to lighten his mood. His thoughts turned to the lesson he'd learned from Pam yesterday, and he decided that sharing it would inject some enthusiasm into his day. He posted on his blog:

> When's the last time the world you thought existed was expanded to a degree that you couldn't imagine? That happened to me yesterday. I was talking with a friend and mentor, Pam, who made a simple comment that shook my view of what my personal network could be. Maybe it's because I'm new to the networking game, and perhaps I should have already known this, but Pam taught me that my network isn't just the people I know—it includes all the

people *they* know. It's everyone I have access to through my own contacts. Who do *you* know who can get things done, for you or for someone you know?

Gnik grabbed a small stack of his business cards, his laptop, and a notepad and stepped out of his apartment building onto the busy street. Without a specific destination in mind, he began walking, dodging the other sidewalk commuters. As he walked, he mulled over the internal conversation he'd had upon awakening.

*I've never really been a people person*, he thought. *I usually get butterflies when I think about meeting someone for the first time. How can I grow my network if I get sweaty palms just going up and starting a conversation?*

Gnik realized he was talking himself out of being successful by dwelling on the "shy" thing. He decided to shift his thinking to something more positive and empowering.

Looking around, he noticed that he'd just passed the entrance to a restaurant he had never seen before. Curious, he entered, picked up a menu, and began studying it. The hostess, an attractive woman dressed in a black pantsuit, walked up to greet him. Smiling, she asked, "Would you like a table, sir?"

"Thanks, I'm just looking for now," he said. "Do you offer takeout?"

She said they were offering takeout but apologized that they hadn't printed their takeout menu yet. "No problem," Gnik said. "How long have you been open?"

"Just two weeks," she said.

"Really? That's great," Gnik offered. "How's business so far?" He realized he was enjoying the conversation and wasn't feeling at all awkward or uncomfortable.

"Slow, but it's starting to pick up," the hostess said. A customer entered the restaurant, and she excused herself to seat him. When she returned, she asked again, "Are you sure you wouldn't like a table?"

"No, thanks. I've already eaten, but I might stop in later. Are you the owner?"

"With my husband, yes."

"Cool!" Gnik beamed, realizing that the self-doubt he had been feeling earlier had completely vanished. He thought, *This is an opportunity to ask some good questions.*

"So, what made you decide to open a restaurant?"

The woman began filling Gnik in on the background of their restaurant, interrupting herself a couple of times to take care of customers. He found himself wondering if he might be able to help with their marketing. *Maybe she'll be my first client,* he thought. He listened intently, and, when she'd finished her story, he took a deep breath.

Drawing on the memory of the networking meeting a couple of days earlier, Gnik reminded himself, *How can she be my client if she doesn't know I exist? That is, if she doesn't know I have a marketing business?* His palms suddenly felt sweaty, but he pushed his feelings of apprehension aside and asked, "Would you be interested in meeting with me to discuss your marketing needs? I've recently started a marketing business, and I'd love to work with you." He looked up expectantly.

# This is an opportunity to ask some good questions.

She smiled and said, somewhat apologetically, "Thank you for offering, but I don't think we're interested. My husband is doing all our marketing, and I think he's got a pretty good handle on things. I do hope you'll stop by for lunch sometime, though."

Gnik felt deflated at the rejection, but he thanked the woman for her time and said he'd come by for a meal one day. He left the restaurant feeling frustrated and wondered what Pam would have done.

As if on cue, his smartphone buzzed. He looked to see a text message from Pam. "Don't take anything personally. Not everything others do is because of you. Hope you're having a great day!"

Gnik smiled and decided to put the restaurant conversation in perspective. *The owner didn't reject my business because she didn't like me; she just doesn't need my services right now.* The thought immediately made him feel better.

He picked up his pace and walked to the library. He wanted a quiet place where he could gather his thoughts and make sure he was focusing on the right things.

Gnik found an empty table in a secluded part of the library. Taking a seat, he began writing in his notepad. At the top of a clean page, he wrote "Tools of the Trade."

# Don't take anything personally.
# Not everything others do is because of you.

He underlined his heading and proceeded to make a list:

- Rejection isn't personal. It's just an indication that my services don't match a potential client's needs.

- When I'm feeling awkward and uncomfortable, the best thing I can do is ask great questions and listen intently.

- People skills can be learned. When all else fails, I can work on my listening skills.

- I need to always be prepared. I never know when an opportunity to talk business will come up.

- Asking great questions empowers others. I could see it in the owner's body language when she began talking about her business.

- Opportunities probably aren't just going to fall into my lap. I need to be assertive in order to get noticed.

- People aren't offended when I assert myself positively.

Gnik left space at the bottom of the page for other ideas that might pop into his head as the day went on. He smiled at the list of lessons he'd been able to extract from his experiences over the past few days. Looking around, he noticed a sign over a bookcase: "Self-Help Books."

He laughed, thinking about how he'd dismissed these types of books before and decided to browse the aisle. *How to Win Friends and Influence People* was prominently displayed on the shelf. As he reached for it, he saw several other books with intriguing titles. He hadn't realized there were so many titles that dealt with developing people skills, though he was starting to appreciate why there would be.

He perused the shelves, selecting a few books that seemed especially relevant or interesting. After checking them out, he headed home, stopping in at the new restaurant he discovered for the second time today, this time to eat.

# Gnik's Aha!

People aren't offended when I assert myself positively. If I am rejected, it only means that there's not a need for my services right now. Not everything others do is because of me.

# The Fastest Way to Connection

Gnik woke up with his head resting on something uncomfortable. He blinked his eyes hard, trying to regain focus. He moved the obstacle off of his pillow and remembered he had been reading in bed last night.

The Dale Carnegie book he'd picked up at the library yesterday was the culprit. Although Gnik felt he understood the basic concepts, he'd started *How to Win Friends and Influence People* after getting into bed the previous night to see if it offered anything he didn't already know.

Fascinated with the wisdom on the pages, he'd read until he fell asleep. Today, he seemed to have awakened with a new perspective. He closed his eyes for a few minutes and pondered some of the events of the past two weeks. He was pleased with how his experiences were coming together, giving him a new understanding about connections.

Gnik hopped out of bed, excited to start the day. He sliced some fruit and poured himself a bowl of granola. He stirred the cereal around in the milk as he sketched out his plans for the day. He decided to call Garrett and see if he was free to meet.

After breakfast, Gnik made the call. On the third ring, a familiar voice announced, "Garrett here."

"Hi, Garrett. It's Gnik—with a G. Can I buy you lunch today?"

"Hello, Gnik. I was just thinking of you. I wish we could connect for lunch, but I've got plans. If you're free for coffee later this afternoon, that would work."

The men coordinated their schedules and hung up. Gnik stuffed his laptop, a notepad, and the Carnegie book into his backpack and set off on the day's adventure.

His first order of business was to purchase a couple of ties. While he'd never been the buttoned-down type, he wanted to make a great impression when approaching potential clients. Most of the businesspeople he'd met here so far, including Pam and Garrett, were sharp dressers, and he wanted to put his best foot forward, too.

Several blocks down in the shopping district, Gnik came upon a promising-looking men's clothing store. He noted the contrast between this shop's stylish storefront and the ones he'd already bypassed. The "Fine Menswear" sign was the first reflection of the elegant mood the store tried to create. Inside, faux marble columns and leather chairs were appropriately placed around the store.

*This place looks expensive,* Gnik thought, confirming his suspicion when he flipped a price tag over. A sales associate, a middle-aged man in a crisp long-sleeved dress shirt, sharply creased pants, and a well-matched tie, walked over.

"Good morning," the man said with a smile as he made eye contact with Gnik.

Gnik returned the pleasant greeting. "Good morning!"

"I'm Keith. What brings you here today?" The salesman maintained steady eye contact, and Gnik was surprised how at ease he felt, especially given his initial concern about prices.

"Hi, Keith, I'm Gnik," he said. "I'm in the market for a couple of ties."

"Welcome, Gnik. I'm sure I can help. Did you have something particular in mind?"

Gnik realized that Keith's communication style was making him feel important as well as comfortable. Even though Keith was no doubt working on commission and was obviously trained to connect with his customers, Gnik found himself enjoying the conversation. "Well, Keith, I'm new to the city, and I've recently started a marketing business. I'm looking for something dignified, professional, not gaudy or pretentious."

"A new marketing business?" Keith inquired. "How is it going?"

"Well, I'm in the very early stages," Gnik said. "I've been developing my network and working on getting my first client."

"Well, if you don't mind me saying so, you have a very professional look about you. I'd expect you to be well received in your business. Let me show you some ideas I have for the perfect tie."

Gnik wondered if the compliment was a ploy to make a sale, but Keith seemed sincerely interested. He followed the salesman to a large display of ties. Ten minutes later, he walked out of the store with two great ties and a level of confidence that made him feel unstoppable.

***

Later that day, as the time for coffee with Garrett approached, Gnik made his way to the designated meeting place. Arriving a few minutes early, he found an open seat, pulled out his book, and was deep in thought when he heard Garrett's voice. "That's one of my favorites. Have you read it before?"

Gnik shook his head as he stood to shake Garrett's hand. "No, I haven't. I picked it up yesterday, and so far it's fascinating."

"So, what can I do for you, Gnik?" Garrett got straight to the point.

Gnik smiled and sat forward in his chair. "Frankly, Garrett, the main reason I called you this morning is no longer a concern, but I appreciate your willingness to meet. May I share my experience with you?"

Garrett agreed, and Gnik recounted his experience buying ties earlier in the day. Garrett gave Gnik a knowing smile, saying, "Have you learned that yet?"

Confused, Gnik looked at Garrett and shrugged his shoulders. "I feel like I'm missing something."

Garrett laughed. "Gnik, you'll find it in the book, and you lived it today. Why did you buy the ties from Keith? I imagine you spent quite a bit more there than you would have at one of the discount outlets."

Gnik just nodded. Garrett raised his eyebrows, waiting for him to answer.

Gnik sat back and looked up at the ceiling, thinking. "Why? Well, I liked the salesman."

"Exactly! People do business with people they like and feel comfortable with. Your decision wasn't about the ties. Now, *why* did you like the salesman?"

## People do business with people they like and feel comfortable with.

"He was pleasant and professional," Gnik said, but as the words came out, he knew there was more to it than that—something he couldn't quite put his finger on.

"Well, you're close," Garrett laughed. "Gnik, the salesman was interested in you. Not in your purchase and not in his commission, but in *you* as a person. You've been to places where the sales staff doesn't want to be bothered, but, today, a salesman took an interest in you. That's it. It really is that simple."

"Wow," Gnik said. "So, that's the secret—it's all about taking a genuine interest in people."

"That's it. Now, it's not always as easy as it sounds, but it's not that hard, either. It also has something to do with the question you asked me the last time we met. Do you remember?"

Gnik squinted, trying to remember. "Sure. I asked about your business card and why you invite people to connect on LinkedIn. Does that have anything to do with my tie shopping experience?"

Garrett laughed again. "More than you'd think, Gnik. I use social media to create a community. Whether it's my company's Facebook page or my professional LinkedIn groups, I want people to feel like they're a part of the community. I want them to be engaged by the questions that are posted. It's fun for me to watch, and I learn a lot about what's going on in their minds. But more importantly, the people who participate have fun engaging with each other, and they like me for giving them the forum. When they like me, they want to do more business with me."

Gnik nodded, seeing even greater power in combining his online networking with his offline efforts.

"Try to create a community yourself, Gnik. Work at it for a few days, then let's get together for lunch."

Garrett stood to leave, and Gnik rose and shook his hand. As Garrett man exited the restaurant, Gnik sat back down, picked up his book, and continued to read about developing great people skills.

# Gnik's Aha!

Being genuinely interested in people makes them feel important and is the fastest way to build strong business and personal connections.

# The 47-Second Networker

Gnik got up feeling that this would be a great day to check out some networking meetings. As he researched nearby meetings he could attend, he noticed some uneasiness building in his gut. He ignored the feeling and wrote down the address of a lunchtime networking group that met just a few blocks away. He also found an interesting service club that was meeting tomorrow. Then he took a deep breath, shook his arms and hands as if trying to throw his discomfort far away, and stepped onto the busy sidewalk outside his apartment building.

Gnik's first task of the day was to go to the library and exchange a couple of books. He had been focusing on his personal strengths and the areas where he recognized he could use some extra help. Time he invested in himself, he knew, would pay big dividends. After selecting several promising titles, he passed through the check-out line and headed over to the lunchtime networking meeting.

Arriving at the meeting, Gnik watched the participants buzz around the room. The flurry of activity reminded him of bees in a hive. A man in a purple button-down shirt and a black tie caught his attention. Gnik grabbed a cup, poured himself a soda, and stood back to watch the purple-shirted man at work.

The man in the purple shirt was far enough away that Gnik could not hear him, but he could imagine the conversations that were taking place. The man didn't stay talking with any one person for long—really just enough to hand out a business card, shake a hand, give a very brief spiel, and move on.

Gnik was so engrossed in the scene that he hadn't noticed the young woman standing next to him. He wondered how long she'd been there.

"Hi, I'm Wendy," she said as he smiled and nodded at her.

"Hello, Wendy. I'm Gnik. Nice to meet you."

"What do you do, Gnik?" Wendy asked as she extended her hand.

Gnik shook her hand firmly. "Well, I moved to the city about two weeks ago, and I've started a marketing business. Things aren't completely off the ground yet, but I'm working on it."

Wendy's eyes darted around the room and landed on someone behind him. Gnik asked Wendy the same question she'd just posed.

Wendy refocused on Gnik. "I'm an interior designer. If you know anyone who can use my services, please send them my way."

As Wendy abruptly walked away, Gnik decided he shouldn't have been surprised that she didn't apparently care to know any more about him. *After all,* he reminded himself, *what she has to say is more important than what I have to say.* He decided to change his approach.

## What she has to say is more important than what I have to say.

Gnik noticed a man in the room who wasn't talking to anyone. He walked over and introduced himself.

"Nice to meet you, Gnik," the man responded. "I'm Roy. What do you do?"

Gnik was a little nervous about trying his unproven technique, but he took a deep breath and forged ahead. "I'm new in town, and I have just started a marketing firm geared toward helping small businesses improve their exposure. But that's enough about me. Tell me a little about yourself, Roy. What do *you* do?"

Gnik was unprepared for the avalanche of information Roy immediately began dumping on him. He looked Roy in the eye the whole time and listened to everything he had to say. Several minutes into the conversation, he had a flash of inspiration.

"So, Roy, as a videographer, I imagine you do weddings?"

"Absolutely," Roy said. "Why? Are you getting married?"

"No," Gnik said, "but I'm wondering if you are connected to a wedding planner or a limo driver, for example."

Roy explained that he got most of his business from small ads in newspapers and the yellow pages, and some customers responded to flyers he distributed around town. "Frankly, Gnik, business is slow. The economy is wiping me out. That's why I've started coming to these things—I'm hoping to meet people who need video work done."

Gnik spent the next couple of minutes explaining the basics of developing a personal network, including, in Roy's case, connecting with people who are already working in the wedding market. "In fact, I know someone who can get that done," he said with a grin. He wrote Pam's contact information on the back of his own business card and handed it to Roy. "I don't believe Pam has a videographer in her network, so there could be a fit. Call her, and let her know I suggested it."

## I know someone who can get that done.

As the two men shook hands and separated, Gnik smiled. *That was fun*, he thought. *And listening to Roy made a big difference.*

He looked around and chose his next contact, a young woman. As he approached her and extended his hand, he said, "Hi, I'm Gnik."

"Hi, Gnik, I'm Olivia. Give me your 47-second spiel."

"Forty-seven seconds?"

Olivia explained, "I've found that it's best to condense your pitch into 47 seconds or less. That's all the time you'll probably have before people try to get the conversation back to themselves. And you'd better make it memorable so their eyes don't glaze over. Here's what I mean. Mine is, 'Hi. I'm Olivia. I'm a mobile DJ, and I bring your choice of music to any party. My business is music to your ears.'"

"Catchy—I like it," Gnik said. "I don't have anything like that yet, but I'll get it figured out."

The two exchanged business cards, and Gnik went on to meet a few more people. He practiced the magic phrase that Pam had taught him, "I know someone who can get that done." He promised to connect online with several of the people he met.

After a satisfying networking experience, Gnik went to the coffee shop, took his favorite seat, and made some social media connections. Then he opened his blog and posted to it, recalling the difference between the man in the purple shirt and Roy:

> I used to think that networking was awkward. A bunch of people passing out business cards and pumping each other for business? I'll pass. But someone challenged me to shift my focus outward. What if I were to reach out to people and just be interested in them, without any expectation of personal gain? This has changed the way I connect with people. Meeting others is more rewarding when I'm focused on *them*.

Gnik looked through the comments on his previous posts. Then, shifting his attention to Olivia's idea, he started to work on his 47-second intro.

# Gnik's Aha!

Most people are more interested in themselves than in me. I need to give a memorable 47-second intro and follow it with, "That's enough about me. What can I do to help you?"

# Personal Flow of Business

When Gnik woke up, he immediately noticed something unusual about the way he was feeling. It wasn't like when he felt networking nerves. And it wasn't so much how refreshed or energized he felt, though there was that. Rather, he had a sense that he was in control of his day. *Well, maybe not in control of my day*, he thought, *but I do feel like I'm in control of myself.*

In his rush to get ready so he wouldn't be late for the service club meeting, Gnik didn't dwell on the new feeling. As he dressed and gathered his things before leaving his apartment, he let his mind reflect on some of the lessons he had learned over the past several days. He reminded himself of several things, such as the importance of listening, taking a personal interest in other people, being noticed, and developing his own personal flow of business. He dropped a stack of business cards into his shirt pocket and then prepared some fruit and cereal for breakfast.

As Gnik ate, he glanced at the notepad lying on the table. Feeling oddly uncomfortable with the blank page, he picked up a pen in his right hand, while still eating breakfast with his left. He almost instinctively wrote the following sentences at the top of the page: "Today, I am developing my personal flow of business. Today, I am growing my network." Gnik read the words several times and found they energized him even further. He hurriedly finished his breakfast and bounded out the door.

The meeting was about a two-mile walk from Gnik's apartment, and he used the time to reflect. *Forty-seven seconds*, he thought. He was intrigued by the concept, and for fun, he posted the three-word status update on Facebook from his smartphone. *Forty-seven seconds.* He suspected that the cryptic update would start some conversations among his friends.

Gnik walked purposefully, his pace quickening as he glanced at his watch. He wanted to get to the meeting early.

At an intersection, while waiting for the light to change, Gnik had a sudden realization. *Purpose*, he thought. *That's what is different today.* He was excited to see how this difference in approach might change the way he experienced networking.

He arrived at the meeting and signed in, writing his name on a name tag. He re-read the sentences on his notepad, reminding himself of his plan. *I'll be looking for opportunities to grow my network, but that doesn't mean I should reject people who don't have an obvious benefit to me or my flow of business.* He was sure there was a way to recognize nuggets of opportunity without turning into the guy in the purple shirt he noticed yesterday—hoping for a great connection and bailing out of the conversation if there didn't seem to be an immediate personal benefit. *After all, even if it seems like they can't help me, I surely can benefit them in some way.*

Gnik glanced around the room. He locked in on a man who was having an animated discussion with another networker. Impressed with his obvious passion for his topic, Gnik approached and waited for an opening. The man, dressed in a dark blue pinstriped suit, stepped back slightly, opening a space for Gnik to join the discussion.

The man looked at Gnik's name tag and extended his hand. "Hi, Gnik. I'm Mark, and this is my new friend, Christine. Please, join us."

After they'd shaken hands all around, Mark asked, "So, Gnik, what do you do?"

Gnik knew this moment was coming and was excited to deliver his 47 seconds. He smiled, stood a little taller, and said, "Thanks for asking, Mark. I'm a business marketing consultant. I do email and mobile marketing. I help small businesses make the most of their marketing dollar." He took a breath and said, "But that's enough about me. I'd love to hear about you."

Smiling, Gnik looked at Christine. He realized he felt genuinely interested in what she had to say.

"Thanks, Gnik," she said. "I'm a web designer. I help companies build an internet presence that reflects their business."

Next, Mark explained that he owned a home healthcare services firm, and that business was really starting to take off.

"In fact, Gnik, I'd love to meet you for coffee sometime to talk about my marketing plan."

## That's enough about me. I'd love to hear about you.

For the next several minutes, Mark and Christine lobbed questions and scenarios at Gnik, asking his opinion on a variety of marketing topics. Gnik enjoyed the interaction and ended up agreeing to meet both Christine and Mark separately. He looked at Christine and, without thinking, asked, "Do you mind if I add you to my personal flow of business?"

Christine seemed confused. "Of course I don't mind, but I'm not sure I understand what you mean."

Gnik realized that most networkers must not be aware of the lesson Pam had taught him about the importance of developing a flow of business. He explained the basic concept to Christine. "I don't have a website yet, so I'd like to work with you to develop one. But even more importantly, as I meet with clients who need help with website design, I'll be happy to send them to you. By the same token, when you come across a client who can use some marketing assistance, I hope you'll send them my way."

Christine chuckled. "That makes perfect sense, Gnik. I'd be honored to join your personal network."

Gnik reached into his pocket and pulled out a cluster of his business cards. Handing them to Christine, he said, "When you find someone, feel free to give them my card. Can I get a few of yours to pass along?"

## Do you mind if I add you to my personal flow of business?

Mark interjected. "I need to get in on this, too." He handed a few cards each to Christine and Gnik. "I realize my work may not mesh as naturally as your businesses do, but it's possible you may meet people who can use my services."

Gnik wrapped up his conversation with Mark and Christine and moved on, meeting a few other people before the scheduled speaker began her presentation. He reflected on the connections he had made and smiled as he realized, *Today, I am developing my personal flow of business. Today, I am growing my network.*

# Gnik's Aha!

It's amazing what can get done when the right group of people come together.

# 15

# The Benefit of Planning

When Gnik woke, he looked out his bedroom window at the flurry of activity on the streets below. After gazing at the scene for a while, he dropped his head back onto his pillow, closed his eyes briefly, and felt grateful for the amazing growth he'd experienced since moving to the city just two short weeks ago. His personal flow of business was starting to come together, and he felt energized by the possibilities.

Gnik checked the comments on his "47 seconds" post and was pleased by what he read. As he'd hoped, it had started a dialogue, including some speculation and confusion over the meaning of his post. He felt it was time to clarify:

> When you meet someone, you probably won't have more than 47 seconds to introduce yourself and give

your pitch. The fact is that most people are more interested in themselves than they are in you, so make your intro brief, then ask about them. Always take the time to listen. When you do, it's easier for people to want to hear more about you.

After having some breakfast, Gnik got down to the work of formulating his plan for the day. He thought a written checklist would keep him focused on his priorities, so he numbered the left side of a blank notebook page and began to fill in the details:

1. Add a graphic designer to my network

2. Close the loop with Pam re: Roy the videographer

Gnik stared at the page while chewing a bite of banana. He realized he had coasted through a lot of days recently and that being purposeful and decisive required a little more focus than he was accustomed to—especially this early in the morning. *Starting the day with a plan is tough,* he thought, *because I have to decide what I will accomplish.*

After clearing the dishes from the table, he picked up his notepad and his backpack. He put the notepad into the pack and dropped his keys and smartphone into his pocket. *I should reconnect with Christine, the website designer, too.* He pulled the pad out and filled in his third item:

3. Formalize connection with Christine

Gnik stepped outside, closed the door behind him, and pulled out his phone to call Pam. He had considered sending her an email with the videographer's information, but he really wanted to meet with her face-to-face. *Pam is smart and savvy, and talking with her energizes and focuses me,* he thought. *I seem to learn something important every time we meet.* She picked up after the first ring, and he asked if they could get together.

"I've got to be somewhere in an hour, but I'm near the coffee shop," she said. "I can meet you there in about 10 minutes, if we can keep it short."

Gnik told her that would be perfect. As he walked to the coffee shop, he pulled from his pocket the stack of business cards he'd been collecting. He leafed through them and found Roy's card from the networking meeting two days ago. Stopping in a store entryway for a moment, he wrote Roy's contact information in his notepad then tucked the card into his shirt pocket. *I need to start asking for at least two cards,* he thought.

He arrived at the coffee shop and sat in his usual spot. Pam hadn't arrived yet, so he pulled out his notepad and contemplated his priorities for the day.

Interrupting his thoughts, Pam took a seat across from him. "How have you been, Gnik?"

"Great!" he beamed, reaching out to give her a firm handshake. Knowing she was short on time, he got right to the point. "You didn't mention anything about having a videographer in your network, and I thought you might want to consider Roy." He pulled Roy's card from his shirt pocket and handed it to Pam. "Seems like a nice guy, very professional. I told him about you and said I'd pass his information along."

Pam took the card and smiled. "Funny you called this morning, Gnik, because I was just thinking about you. I know someone who might be able to help *you* out. Her name's Yvonne, and she runs a printing company. I've used her for some of my mailers, and she does excellent work." She gave Gnik the printer's contact info.

## I need to start asking for at least two cards.

Gnik looked at his list and put his pen on his Item 1. "Oh, so close," he said with a wistful grin. He moved the pen to the bottom of the list and wrote:

4. Add Yvonne, the printer, to my business network

Pam looked at the list curiously. "What's that all about?"

"I've figured out that I can get more accomplished when I put the day's priorities in writing. So, this is today's list. You're on there—Item 2." He gave her a wink and a smile. "No offense, Pam, but I can cross you off now."

Pam shot Gnik a look of mock insult and then asked, "What do you mean with that third item, 'Formalize connection with Christine'?"

"That was sort of a fleeting thought," Gnik said, a bit embarrassed to have Pam analyzing his list and probably finding it terribly simplistic. "I met Christine yesterday at a service club meeting. She's a web designer—a very good one, from what I've seen—and I asked her if I could add her to my personal network. I had to explain the flow of business to her, just like you explained it to me. She agreed, but I had the thought today that I should reconnect with her, thank her for the conversation, and reaffirm that I want to include her in my personal flow of business. But now I'm thinking it's a pretty dumb idea." He began to cross Item 3 off the list.

Pam pushed his pen off the paper and covered the list with her hand. "Stop, Gnik. You're underestimating the value of this idea." She moved her hand off the notepad. "How many times has someone followed up to affirm the initial connection they made with you? It's rare, and it's a really smart idea, so keep it on your list. Formalize that connection with Christine. I have a feeling it could turn out very well."

## I can get more accomplished when I put the day's priorities in writing.

With that, Pam apologized that she had to run. She thanked him for Roy's card and reminded him to call Yvonne. "She's expecting to hear from you, Gnik," she said as she departed with a wave and a smile.

Gnik pulled out his laptop and flipped through the business cards again, this time looking for Christine's information. He wrote a short email:

Christine,

It was a true pleasure meeting you at the service club meeting yesterday. I enjoyed getting to know you, and I'm looking forward to working with you in the future.

I checked out some of your work, and I'm impressed. I plan to refer my clients who need web design services to you. If you have clients who need help with their marketing, I hope you won't hesitate to send them my way.

Thanks again, and let's get together for coffee soon so we can strategize.

Gnik

*"Making the most of your marketing dollar"*
*~ Connect with me on LinkedIn*
*~ Friend me on facebook.com/GnikRowten*
*~ Follow me on Twitter @GnikRowten*

After sending the message, Gnik connected with Christine through social networks as well, then sat back and took a deep breath. He crossed Item 3 off his list. Now, he just needed to find a graphic designer and call the printer Pam had recommended. It was still early in the day.

Gnik decided to start with Yvonne, thinking that as a printer she might be able to recommend a graphic designer. He opened his notepad to a fresh page and dialed the number Pam had given him. Yvonne answered the phone pleasantly and laughed when he said he was calling because Pam had suggested they connect.

"I can't tell you how rare it is that someone actually calls," she said, chuckling.

Gnik and Yvonne chatted for several minutes, and Gnik offered to stop by her print shop so they could meet in person. They agreed to meet that afternoon.

\*\*\*

Gnik arrived at Yvonne's print shop at the appointed hour and waited while the owner wrapped up a conversation with a customer. She asked how she could help him, and he smiled and offered his hand.

"Hi, Yvonne, I'm Gnik, Pam's friend. Is now still a good time?"

"Great to meet you, Gnik!" she enthused. "Please have a seat and make yourself comfortable." She grabbed a bottle of water from the small refrigerator and handed it to Gnik.

Gnik looked at the samples posted around the shop. "Pam was right," he said. "You do great work." Yvonne smiled and sat down.

"So," she began, "how can we help each other?"

Gnik explained his idea of forming a natural flow of business that would benefit them both. He suggested having an informal meeting tomorrow where the group could come together, get acquainted, and discuss his concept and the possibilities. His notepad reminded him to ask, "Do you happen to know a good graphic designer?"

Yvonne laughed. "Do I know a designer? You bet! My closest friend is the best in town. She does a lot of work for me."

Gnik grinned. Things seemed to be coming together beautifully. "Would you mind asking if she could join us tomorrow?"

"Of course," Yvonne exclaimed. "She'll be there!"

The two brainstormed some other functions that seemed to fit and shared the names of people who might make a useful contribution to the group. Yvonne offered her back room for the meeting, and they agreed on the other details. As he headed back home, Gnik knew he was starting to experience the power of networking to create a personal flow of business. *Pam was right!* he thought. *My network doesn't stop at the people I know; it includes all the people I have access to.* After reviewing the notes from his meeting with Yvonne, he started contacting all the people he hoped to bring together tomorrow.

# Gnik's Aha!

I will approach my day with a plan. I will find success as I decide what I want to accomplish and then look for opportunities to move in that direction.

# day 16

# Network With Abundance

Gnik woke up before his smartphone alarm rang, and, in the darkness, he listened to the sounds of the early morning. The traffic on the street below his window was beginning to come alive, and he could hear the unmistakable sounds of the city waking up.

Hopping out of bed, he grabbed his notepad and smartphone and dropped them on the kitchen table. He had a lot of work to do this morning.

After his shower, Gnik wiped the steam off the bathroom mirror and stared at his reflection. "Hi, I'm Gnik Rowten, your marketing consultant. I help businesses like yours make the most of their marketing dollar." Gnik felt a little silly talking to his own reflection, but he wanted to get the words imprinted on his subconscious so that when he was asked about himself, they would just come out naturally.

"Hi, I'm Gnik Rowten, your marketing consultant. I help businesses like yours make the most of their marketing dollar." The ringing of Gnik's smartphone interrupted his third attempt. He pulled his shirt on as he rushed to answer the phone.

"Hi, Gnik. It's Yvonne. Just following up."

"Hey, Yvonne! It was great meeting you yesterday. I'm really looking forward to working with you."

"Same here, Gnik," she said with enthusiasm. "I'm looking forward to working with you, too!"

They updated one another on who would be attending the group meeting today, and Yvonne shared her thoughts about the agenda. "A question, Gnik ... I hope I wasn't out of line, but I had dinner with my friend Gail last night—she's like a sister to me, and she's a social media master. We started talking business, and I told her about you and your networking concept. She said she'd love to be involved, and I invited her to meet with us today. She really brings a lot to the table with her social media expertise—what do you think?"

Gnik's immediate reaction was to feel threatened. Social media marketing would be a natural component of his own service offerings, and now it seemed he was about to come face-to-face with a potential competitor.

The lengthy pause on his end of the line was uncomfortable for Yvonne, and she quickly backpedaled. "I'm sorry about that, Gnik—I should have checked with you first. I'll just let her know we need to reschedule."

Not wanting to disappoint his new friend, Gnik assured Yvonne that while she'd taken him a bit by surprise, he'd welcome Gail's participation. *This ought to be interesting,* he thought.

"Are you sure, Gnik?"

"I'm positive, Yvonne," he said. "It'll be great. Having someone who understands social media strategy will be a plus. I'm looking forward to it." He almost believed himself.

After the two had hung up, Gnik looked at his notes from yesterday:

**My Personal Flow of Business**
Yvonne – Graphic Printing
Jan (Yvonne's friend) – Graphic Design
Christine – Website Design
Gnik – Marketing Strategist
Rachel – Copywriting
Kim – 3D Digital Artist

Now he added Yvonne's other friend to the list:

Gail – Social Media

Gnik knew he would need to be selective about the people he included in his personal flow. He didn't want to risk embarrassment and even potential loss of business by having a partner who produced inferior work. He had seen Christine's work, and he was comfortable with Pam's recommendation of Yvonne. *Still,* he thought, *we need to be sure to vet the people we add to our group.*

In spite of this very practical concern, as Gnik looked over the list, he found himself thinking, *This could be a powerful team.* Not only that, but his feelings of insecurity in respect to Gail's involvement had vanished completely. After all, he'd decided, given his own somewhat superficial knowledge of social media marketing strategy, it made sense to welcome an expert rather than feel threatened.

The meeting time finally came, and as the invited individuals began to arrive at Yvonne's print shop, Gnik greeted each of them warmly, presenting them with a beverage and a name tag that included their first names and business specialties. He made a point of introducing each individual to everyone else in the group. After everyone had arrived, he gave the group several minutes to chat and mingle before calling the meeting to order.

"I want to thank all of you for taking the time to come here this afternoon, and on very short notice," Gnik began. "I'd like to start this first meeting by explaining what Yvonne and I are trying to accomplish." He gestured to Yvonne, whose cue it was to take over.

"Gnik shared something with me when we met yesterday, and I thought it was important enough to act on it right away. Just as when we see our own doctor and he refers us to a specialist, we can act as doctor and specialist for one another. Our purpose today is to invite you to become a part of our natural flow of business. First, we need to make sure we're all connected on Facebook and LinkedIn. Beyond that, the idea is to use our mutual connections to grow our businesses and enhance the services we provide to our customers."

"I'd like to give you an example of how this works," Gnik said, his eyes sparkling with excitement as he picked up the narrative. "I recently met a gentleman who owns and operates a home healthcare company, providing care to homebound seniors and invalids. He needs help with his marketing, and I've agreed to meet with him in a few days. As I look at his marketing strategy, I may find that he needs better copywriting on his direct mail pieces, so I would like to refer him to you, Rachel. If I learn that he has a particular need in the area of social media, I'll make recommendations and subcontract the work to you, Gail. If this works like it does in doctors' offices, we should all see a benefit."

"As long as we are willing to share with each other," Yvonne declared.

Gnik paused to let the idea sink in. Gail raised her hand slightly, and Gnik asked if she had a question.

"If I understand you correctly," Gail started, "we can either pass business directly to each other, or we can take on the project ourselves and subcontract the work to someone in the group?"

"That's exactly right, Gail," Gnik said. "There are different and equally valid ways to share the work, and the referring individual will suggest the solution that makes the most sense to him or her given the particular circumstances. The key, really, is remembering to use the eight magic words of networking: 'I know someone who can get that done.'"

Kim spoke up next. "What do you propose in cases where a client needs something that nobody in this group can provide?"

"I'm really glad you asked that question, Kim," Gnik said. "First, remember that your network isn't just the people you know. It includes *everyone* you have access to. You'll want to be the expert for your client—always. To accomplish that, you can reach out, any time, to anyone in this group or, indeed, to the group itself. Between us, and that includes our extended networks, we should be able to identify the right resource or solution for virtually any client need."

"That's right," Yvonne said. "There's an abundance of talent that we can quickly and easily access."

"*Abundance*—I like that word," Rachel reflected. "I think you're right, Gnik and Yvonne. If I start thinking of things from an abundant mindset ...." Her voice trailed off.

## Use the eight magic words of networking: "I know someone who can get that done."

"No doubt there are plenty of people out there whom we can help and who can help us," Jan offered, "and working together like this will only give us access to more of them. I have to admit that when Yvonne first mentioned the idea, I was worried that you all might try to steal my customers, but from what I'm hearing, the point is the exact opposite."

Gnik's smile betrayed the fact that he had shared Jan's concern earlier in the day. He reassured the group. "Jan is right. We can help and collaborate with each other. We don't have to compete."

An idea was forming in Gnik's head, even as he realized that this new group saw him as an expert networker. He paused before continuing. "In fact, we could easily expand this group into a referral exchange. Are any of you familiar with the concept?"

He looked around and saw a couple of nods, but most of the group seemed confused.

Yvonne spoke up. "A business referral group meets regularly for the purpose of exchanging referrals. Right now, we have one copywriter, one web designer, and so forth. I think Gnik's suggesting that we invite some of our other business contacts to future meetings, which would focus on referring business within the group. Am I understanding you, Gnik?"

## We can help and collaborate with each other. We don't have to compete.

Gnik agreed, and the individuals in the group nodded their approval. They confirmed each other's contact information, and Gnik explained the idea of being a 47-second networker. "I think we should share our 47 seconds with each other, and if that includes a memory hook, that makes it even better.

**111**

Mine is, 'Hi, I'm Gnik Rowten, your marketing consultant. I help businesses like yours make the most of their marketing dollar."

Jan began laughing. "I have a memory hook, but I never thought of calling it that! It has worked pretty well for me, though."

Gnik smiled and asked Jan to share. "Let's hear it. It will make it easier for us to understand what we can do for each other."

Jan stood and proudly explained, "I'm Jan MacDougall, and I'll help you with your graphic design needs. When you need to illustrate your point, don't Google it … MacDougall it!"

Gnik laughed and agreed that Jan had a great memory hook. The other members of the newly formed group shared the details of what they brought to the group.

Gnik sat back and enjoyed the moment. *It's phenomenal to see the energy and power that comes from having the right group of people working together.*

# Gnik's Aha!

There's no shortage of people I can count on or that I can help. As I grow my personal flow of business, my network will grow, and my business will benefit.

day **17**

# The Importance of Following Up

It was still dark out as Gnik headed to the gym for a quick early morning workout. As he ran on the treadmill, he focused on the pounding sound his feet made each time they made contact with the belt beneath him. He let the rhythmic sound distract him from work-related matters. For now, he just wanted to relax his brain and work out his body.

After a vigorous run, Gnik wrapped up his workout by lifting weights and sitting in the sauna. Alone in the steam room, he thought about the things he wanted to get done today. After showering and getting dressed, he returned home to solidify his plans. On his way into the apartment, he checked his mailbox, pulling out a stack of letters, magazines, and junk mail. He leafed through them as he walked up the stairs, taking special note of an envelope addressed to him in his grandmother's handwriting. *Probably my birthday card and check*, he thought, though his birthday was still a week away.

Gnik's grandmother had long ago started a tradition of sending each grandchild a card on his or her birthday with a check for as many dollars as the grandchild's age. Without any announcement, she had apparently decided at some point to cap the size of the gift. According to the check, Gnik was still eighteen.

He smiled as he read the personal note Grandma had written on the card and then tucked the check into his wallet. He decided to send her a thank-you card now, rather than putting it off until some vague point in the future. After he'd written his note and addressed and stamped the envelope, he reflected on the many lessons his mother had taught him as he grew up. He realized that the etiquette he had learned was becoming rare. He pulled out a second thank-you card and wrote a quick note to his mother, expressing appreciation for the good manners and habits she'd instilled in him as a child.

Gnik gathered up his notes from yesterday, his laptop, and his outgoing mail, and got ready to leave. Without really thinking about it, he tossed his remaining supply of thank-you cards into his backpack and then navigated his way to the coffee shop for a cup of java and a short planning session.

As he walked, Gnik reflected on the very positive and productive meeting he and Yvonne had held with their startup "personal flow of business" group. He realized how grateful he was for the connections he'd been making over the past few days, and though he still wasn't completely certain what he wanted to accomplish today, he knew he'd figure it out.

At the coffee shop, Gnik placed his order, scanning the customers as he patiently waited for his coffee, imagining the important business that was taking place. Thinking back to the conversations he'd had here with Pam, he was amazed at the importance this little room had already played in his own business. He thought about his good luck in having met Pam just over two weeks ago.

Gnik took his coffee and placed a tip in the jar. He settled into an open seat and pulled out his blank thank-you cards, intending to write a note to Pam. While he had already expressed his gratitude to her in person and via email, his mother's words echoed: *Never underestimate the power of a thank-you note. People appreciate the effort.* He wrote a heartfelt note of gratitude for the ideas, recommendations, and suggestions Pam had given him over the last couple of weeks.

It occurred to Gnik that it would be a nice touch to send an appreciative follow-up note to everyone in his new personal flow of business team. He started with Yvonne and then wrote a short note each to Jan, Christine, Kim, Gail, and Rachel.

Gnik finished writing the cards and shook the cramp from his hand. As he sat in the coffee shop with the completed stack of cards in front of him, he remembered what Pam had said about follow-up at this same table just two days earlier: "It's a really smart idea. Formalize that connection ... it could turn out very well."

## Never underestimate the power of a thank-you note. People appreciate the effort.

He sat back in his chair, realizing he hadn't paid close enough attention to that nugget of wisdom from Pam. Yes, he'd reached out to Christine a couple of days ago to affirm their connection, but he hadn't thought about following up with *all* his recent contacts.

Taking the stack of business cards he'd been accumulating out of his backpack, Gnik looked through them and then wrote a short email message to each person in turn. Wherever possible, he included small details that personalized the messages, but the basic wording was the same:

> I truly enjoyed meeting you, and I look forward to interacting with you as part of my network. I've also invited you to connect with me on Facebook and LinkedIn, which will help us stay connected.

Gnik reflected on the fact that none of the people he'd met and swapped cards with had followed up with *him*, and briefly wondered if he was making a mistake. Again, he remembered his mother's words, *Never underestimate the power of a thank-you note.* He continued to work at it until he'd sent a message to everyone he had a card for, and then sat back and smiled. Going back through the stack of cards, he requested Facebook and LinkedIn connections with each of them. As he did, he was reminded of Garrett's observation: *I can't have too many friends.*

## I truly enjoyed meeting you, and I look forward to interacting with you as part of my network.

A follow-up email message wasn't a cure for everything, Gnik knew, and he also realized that not everyone would accept his request to connect, but he believed that making an effort to reconnect with people—even those he'd just met—could only strengthen his connections and enhance his network.

As he walked back to his apartment, Gnik decided that following up to reconnect would be a regular part of his networking strategy moving forward. *It's not that hard, but it's also not that common. I think it will make a difference,* he thought.

# Gnik's Aha!

Following up with everyone I meet is a powerful way to formalize relationships and build a better network.

day **18**

# Act as the Host

Gnik opened his eyes when the alarm rang and stretched his legs under the weight of the comforter. They still ached from yesterday's workout, but stretching them was energizing. He flexed his ankles and stretched his calves. As the increased blood circulation gradually woke him up, he pushed the covers aside and stood on the cool floor. Today was sure to be another exciting day.

Eager to reinforce the lesson he'd learned yesterday, Gnik posted to his blog, offering a challenge to his readers:

> When's the last time you got a thank-you card? Not an email or a text, but an actual physical card? In the *mail*? These days, it's unusual for people to follow up, so when you do, you will stand out. Follow up

relentlessly. Don't wait too long. Should you send a card or an email? Why not do both?

After dressing, Gnik went to his fridge and was disappointed to realize it was largely empty. *Time to stock up*, he figured. He grabbed his jacket, wallet, and keys, and double-checked that he had his grocery loyalty card.

Twenty minutes later, as he approached the store entrance, Gnik was lost in thought, imagining the succulent meals he would prepare with today's food acquisition. He entered the store, nearly bumping into the sweetly enthusiastic woman who stood at the front door, acting as if her purpose in life was to give each customer a cheerful greeting.

"Welcome! Would you like a cart?"

Shaken from his trance, Gnik nodded and accepted the cart she was offering.

"Enjoy your shopping trip!" she called after him. He smiled, thinking, *It's great to see someone so excited about her job.*

Gnik moved methodically through the aisles in search of the items on his list. His shopping nearly complete, he stopped to compare labels on two large bottles of multivitamins. He selected one and dropped it into his cart before finally reaching the checkout line. At the store exit, he nearly bumped into the same happy woman who had welcomed him into the store.

"Did you find everything you were looking for?" she asked with a smile.

Gnik nodded, returning the smile.

"Great!" she said, opening the door for Gnik. "Thanks for shopping with us, and I hope we'll see you back here soon!"

The brief interaction somehow boosted Gnik's mood. As he made his way toward his apartment, he found himself walking a little taller, and he smiled and nodded to most of the people he passed. To those who made eye contact, he offered a friendly "Hello."

Gnik hurriedly put his groceries away and headed back outside. The weather was perfect, and he was looking forward to spending a few relaxing hours at the park.

Humming to himself, he walked through the park, remembering a conversation he'd had with Pam a couple of weeks earlier. *Happiness is a switch*, he recalled her saying—and how right she was! The contemplative moment was suddenly interrupted by the deep vibrations of bells ringing in the church just across the road from him. He stood and enjoyed the bell concert for a few minutes before deciding to enter the church to continue his afternoon of reflection and gratitude.

Gnik was a little apprehensive about entering the sanctuary, but as he approached the door, a friendly looking older man walked up to him, smiling.

"Good afternoon and welcome to the church," he said. "I'm James. May I show you around?"

Gnik shook James's hand and introduced himself. The two walked to the front of the sanctuary, where James explained the significance of some of the artifacts on display. "I don't believe I've seen you here before, Gnik. You're not a member, are you?" James asked.

"No, I'm not, actually," Gnik said. "I was in the park when the bells started ringing. I thought I'd stop in and enjoy the peace I knew I'd find here."

James gave Gnik a knowing smile. "It *is* a peaceful place, indeed. I'll show you where you can sit and have a few moments to yourself."

The older man led Gnik to a secluded part of the sanctuary, where he would be out of the way of any foot traffic but still able to enjoy the marvelous architecture and stained glass.

"Why don't you let me take your coat? I'll hang it on the rack near the door. Take your time. I hope you enjoy your moment of peace."

Gnik removed his jacket and handed it to James, who left him to his thoughts. He sat in the pew and leaned his head back, taking in the grandeur as he pondered the significant events of the past few weeks. He recalled his fortuitous first meeting with Pam and his conversation with Garrett about the value of great questions. He reflected on the importance of being noticed and of following up with others. Memories of these and other revelatory moments swirled in his head as he closed his eyes to focus his thoughts.

Gnik thought of the woman he'd met at the grocery store earlier. *She's got this stuff nailed*, he thought. He remembered how his interaction with her had made him feel. In a vast store in an unfamiliar city, Gnik had felt like he was a regular. *How did she do that?*

Then his thoughts flipped to James, and their short conversation just moments ago. *James did it, too. I feel like this is* my *church, though it's my first visit.*

Gnik let those two experiences dominate his attention, realizing that if he could capture what the grocery store lady and James had done, he'd be able to implement it in his network and his business. He was having a hard time putting his finger on it, when James walked by.

**He recalled his fortuitous first meeting with Pam and his conversation with Garrett about the value of great questions. He reflected on the importance of being noticed and of following up with others.**

"I don't mean to bother you," the older man said, "but I'm afraid I've been a poor host. I've brought you some water." Smiling, he handed Gnik a bottle of water.

"I really appreciate your hospitality, James," Gnik said, accepting the bottle. "Are you the pastor?"

"No," James said, waving his hand. "I'm just a member who wants to make sure everyone has as great an experience here as I have. I'll get out of your way now. Enjoy your visit."

Gnik snapped his fingers. *That's it! They have no formal authority or responsibility to ensure I have a great experience; they've just taken it upon themselves to be good hosts.*

He grinned as the possibilities flooded his mind. *Networking meetings will never be the same. I'll act as host— letting others feel like honored guests.*

Gnik stood and thanked James for the wonderful introduction to the church. He retrieved his jacket and went outside, eager for the next opportunity where he could serve as a host.

# Gnik's Aha!

When I interact with people, I can turn an unremarkable experience into a memorable one by acting as the host. I want to make sure their needs are being met.

# Become Fascinated

The air was cold on Gnik's face, so he pulled the covers over his head. Deciding he could warm up just as easily by getting showered and dressed, he gritted his teeth and stepped onto the cold hardwood floor. He waited for the steam to fill the shower and then entered, letting the hot water cascade over his face.

For breakfast, Gnik opted for a trip to the coffee shop rather than digging into his newly acquired kitchen stash. He gathered the tools he expected to use, especially his notepad, and navigated to the coffee shop. Entering, he noticed the place was hopping. He placed his usual coffee order, added a jumbo pastry, and settled into a chair at one of the few available tables.

As Gnik ate, he was thinking about his trip home for his friend Samantha's wedding in just a few days. Creating an online event, he invited The Crew to get together while he was in town.

He thought about yesterday, and he wondered how he might be able to act like a host in a general setting—in a coffee shop, for example. He was gazing out the window and considering his options when he noticed a young mother, juggling a toddler, an infant, and a couple of shopping bags, struggling to get through the door. Instinctively, he hopped up and held the door open for her. She graciously accepted his gesture, and he returned to his corner seat to consider how he could act as host. Suddenly, it hit him that he had just done exactly that, which made him laugh out loud. *I guess there really are opportunities everywhere*, he thought.

Gnik settled into his personal planning session, feeling more confident that he could, in fact, act like a host in almost any situation. Barely a minute had gone by when he was approached by a young man, probably a couple of years younger than himself, professionally dressed in tan slacks and a white button-down shirt, with a black tie hanging loose around his neck.

"Do you mind if I sit here?" The young man had a few books and a laptop in his arms.

"Be my guest," Gnik responded.

The young man sat down and extended his hand. "I'm Patrick."

"Gnik. What are you working on?"

"I sell insurance part time while I'm in school. Trying to pay the bills, but it's a tough market out there. Nobody's buying."

"Really?" Gnik was surprised. "I guess I'm not up to speed on the insurance industry. What type of policies do you sell?"

"Mostly life, but sometimes I'll sell a health policy." Patrick pulled out his smartphone to respond to a text message.

## I guess there really are opportunities everywhere.

Gnik was curious. "Tell me about your life policies."

Patrick hurriedly explained the basic whole life and term life policies he handled, but from the quick summary, Gnik didn't fully grasp the difference between the two. "Would you mind answering some questions I have about insurance, or is this not a good time for you?"

"No, go ahead." Patrick didn't look up from his phone.

Gnik explained that he was currently uninsured. Did Patrick think there were some worthwhile options Gnik, as a young, unmarried man should consider?

Patrick continued to focus on his phone. Then his eyes darted around the coffee shop as if he were looking for someone. Gnik wasn't sure he'd heard his question.

After an uncomfortable pause, Patrick responded generically. "Yeah, you should look into it."

Gnik felt that continuing the conversation would be awkward, so he turned his focus back to his daily plan. Patrick finished his coffee, put his phone in his pocket, and stood to leave.

Patrick dropped his card on the table in front of Gnik and stacked up his books. "When you're interested in talking more about your insurance needs, give me a call."

Gnik picked up the card and nodded. "Thanks. It was nice meeting you."

Patrick walked out the door, and Gnik reflected on the conversation. He rummaged through his bag in search of his stack of business cards. Remembering that he had recently met someone who sold life insurance, he flipped through the cards until he came across Izzy's. He sat back in his chair and studied the two cards in his hand.

*Both Patrick and Izzy sell insurance, and although they both seem like nice guys, given a choice between the two, I'd have to go with Izzy.* Gnik considered what made him feel this way and recalled that Izzy seemed to be really passionate about insurance. Still, he didn't feel that "passion" accounted for the full difference between the two.

Gnik flipped the cards over in his hands, reading the note he'd written to himself on the back of Izzy's card. *Needs help with marketing.* He remembered the story Izzy had told him, and the feelings he'd had during the conversation flooded his mind.

*Izzy was interested in* me. *He asked questions about me. He seemed fascinated about what I might be able to do to help him. Patrick, on the other hand, didn't seem to have* any *interest in me or my business. The work I do never even came up.*

Gnik remembered the shopping trip to buy a tie. He realized that, once again, he was choosing to pursue a business relationship based on liking one person more than another. *Yes, the biggest difference,* he decided, *is that Izzy was interested in me, while Patrick acted like I was an interruption.*

### He realized that, once again, he was choosing to pursue a business relationship based on liking one person more than another.

Gnik realized that if he chose to connect with people based on how interested they were in listening to him, he could improve his business relationships by being more interested in others. He picked up the phone, dialed Izzy's number, and asked, "Can we get together to talk about insurance?"

# Gnik's Aha!

When I become fascinated with other people and listen intently, I get to enjoy the interaction.

# day 20

# Listen to Their Stories

*This is a tie day,* Gnik decided as he examined the ties in his closet. He made a selection that he thought was both classy and bold. As he knotted the fabric around his neck and glanced at the stack of business cards on his dresser, he chided himself. Yes, he'd sent thank-you notes to the people these cards represented a few days ago, but he hadn't done anything else to solidify his networking relationship with them. *Today's the day I'll reach out to the people I've met,* he told himself.

As he mentally planned the conversations he would have, Gnik felt fortunate, even blessed, that they were willing to be a part of his network.

*Maybe I'll throw a party,* he considered. *I wonder if people would show up if I called it a "Networking Thank-You Event?"*

He chuckled. Expressing gratitude to his network struck him as a great concept, and he immediately began making plans. First, he looked at the calendar to find a date that would give him time to properly prepare and invite his guests. As he selected a few options, it occurred to him that something spontaneous in the meantime would be worthwhile and fun, if he could pull it off.

## Today's the day I'll reach out to the people I've met.

*I'll just throw it out there and see if anyone is free for an informal get-together tomorrow afternoon,* he decided. He'd gotten to know the couple who owned the restaurant down the street pretty well over the last couple of weeks, and since business was a bit slow, he thought they might be able to accommodate a private party in their back room on short notice. He rang the restaurant and reached Wanda, who owned and operated it with her husband, Guy.

"Hi, Wanda, it's Gnik Rowten. If you can swing it, I'd love to have a small business networking group in for a meeting there tomorrow afternoon—ideally in that great back room of yours." Wanda was enthusiastic. The two worked out the details, and it was even agreed that Wanda and Guy would take part if the restaurant wasn't too busy.

Next, Gnik flipped through his stack of cards, mentally counting the contacts he'd made. While he had been planning to invite everyone, he thought this might be a good time to prioritize his contacts. He separated the cards into several piles. The first group included the people to whom he'd sent a thank-you card and who had responded to his Facebook and LinkedIn invitations. These were the people he was actively connected to and were his core contacts at this point, he figured. The second pile included the people to whom he'd reached out to on Facebook or LinkedIn but had yet to receive a response from. The third stack represented people he'd met recently but not yet followed up with.

Gnik picked up the third stack of cards and flipped through them a couple of times, trying to remember each individual. Unfortunately, he realized he had forgotten many of them, so he separated these cards into two stacks, reflecting the people he remembered and those he didn't.

He picked up the small pile of cards from people he couldn't remember and held them over the trash can for several seconds as he rationalized tossing them. A couple of the cards slipped from his fingers but landed on the floor instead of in the trash.

Gnik picked the cards up off the floor and looked at them again. Feeling guilty for having considered throwing them away, he squared the stack again. *Why should I exclude people from my network just because I can't remember them? You never know—one or more of them could turn out to be important.*

Gnik put the "can't remember" pile alongside the "remember but haven't followed up yet" pile. Reminding himself to think of his network with an "abundance" mindset, Gnik arranged the cards in front of him. Picking up the stack of cards of people he remembered but had yet to follow up with,

Gnik looked at the top card. His thoughts flashed back to the bus ride a couple of weeks ago. Gnik dialed the number on the card.

"Hi Evan, this is Gnik Rowten. I'm not sure you'll remember me, but we met on the bus a couple of weeks ago. You offered to connect me with a guitar teacher."

It took Evan a moment to place Gnik, but then he said, "Sure, I remember. I was on my way to the hospital to visit my grandmother."

Gnik paused. He felt awkward diving right into his invitation to tomorrow's gathering. "I'm sorry to hear about that, Evan," he said. "I hope she's okay."

"Thanks. She's out of the hospital and doing a lot better now, but she was having a tough time the day you saw me. She loves listening to my guitar, so I was going there to try to cheer her up."

## Why should I exclude people from my network just because I can't remember them?

Gnik realized he was naturally interested in what Evan had to say; it wasn't a matter of trying to fake it or reminding himself to demonstrate his interest.

Evan offered a few more details about his grandmother before pausing, as if suddenly realizing that Gnik had probably called for some purpose. "Sorry to have rambled on, Gnik.

What can I do for you? Did you want me to connect you with my friend who teaches guitar?"

"I'm not quite ready for that yet," Gnik said, "though I'm thinking about it. The reason I called is to invite you to a gathering I'm having tomorrow afternoon. I know it's short notice, and I'll be inviting you to a more formal networking event in about a month, but in the meantime, I've met so many amazing people since I moved here that I just wanted to reconnect, bring them all together, and say thanks."

Evan sounded intrigued, so Gnik shared the details of the meeting. He added, "And please bring your guitar, if you think you might like to play a few songs."

After hanging up with Evan, Gnik relaxed for a moment. *I didn't realize how quickly I could forget someone or vice versa. If I hadn't followed up with Evan, it would be as if we'd never met, and that would have been a shame.*

**I didn't realize how quickly I could forget someone or vice versa. If I hadn't followed up, it would be as if we'd never met.**

Gnik allowed this realization to sink into his mind. He then took Evan's card and set it aside. *One down, lots to go!* He dialed the number on the second card.

His second conversation was similar to the first, though the details were obviously different. Steve instantly remembered Gnik as the Good Samaritan who had helped him change his flat tire a few weeks earlier. Gnik spent most of the call listening to Steve talk about automotive problems, and, again, he found himself enjoying the conversation. Steve promised to attend Gnik's get-together.

Gnik finished making calls to the people he had only met casually and then moved on to Yvonne and the other people in his personal flow of business network. Finally, he called Garrett and Pam, both of whom appeared flattered to be invited and very supportive of the concept.

Next, Gnik created an online event invitation and sent it to all of his new contacts. He included both the people he had actually talked to over the phone and those he'd been unable to reach. *After all, I can't follow up too much.* After finishing the details on the event page, he leaned back in his chair, closed his eyes, and let out a deep sigh.

From an informal analysis of his calls, Gnik recognized a similar structure to the conversations. *Listening certainly is the key,* he realized. *When I listen to their stories—the whole story—first, then it seems they're ready to really listen to me and take what I have to say seriously.*

Gnik decided there should be no structured agenda for tomorrow's meeting. A few friends, a couple drinks, and some food were all they'd need. Still, he did want to announce the more formal party he planned to hold in a month or so, and that meant there was work to be done. He grabbed his notebook, wrote "Gnik's Gratitude Networking Event" at the top of the first blank page, and started a to-do list. *I've got a lot of work ahead of me,* he said out loud to his apartment walls.

# Gnik's Aha!

When I listen—*really* listen to the other person's story, the whole story—that person will listen more carefully to what I have to say *and* take it more seriously.

# day 21

# The Gathering

Early in the morning, Gnik realized he wasn't quite asleep, but he wasn't quite awake either. In this wistful, dream-like state, Gnik imagined a string wrapping around people, connecting them to other people, until everyone was linked to everyone else in a web of connections. He could see the vast network that held everyone together. He smiled at the thought of being connected in such a personal way to so many other people. As he blinked his eyes, the scene faded and he woke up fully with the realization of the important task at hand.

Gnik hopped out of bed and hurriedly prepared himself to leave his apartment for the day. He still had a lot of planning to do before his upcoming Gratitude Event, but he'd gotten the basics confirmed and now his primary focus was on the informal gathering he had arranged for this afternoon.

At the restaurant, as Gnik helped Wanda set up for the event, he thought back to his first visit here a few weeks earlier, realizing how much his mindset had changed in just that short amount of time. That first time, when Wanda had declined his services, he'd taken it quite personally, in spite of some words of wisdom from Pam. But, today, he just felt grateful to have developed a connection that enabled him to host a gathering of his new friends at the restaurant. By scheduling the meeting room for the restaurant's slowest time—after the lunch hour—he hoped Wanda and Guy would be able to stop in.

When the appointed hour arrived and the invitees began filtering in, Gnik greeted them with a warm smile, a name tag, and a word of thanks. In addition to pointing out the plentiful assortment of appetizers and beverages, he went out of his way to introduce each new arrival to at least one other person.

While the guests mingled, Gnik mixed with the group himself, noting a couple of wallflowers and drawing them into conversations. After about 20 minutes of chatting and networking, he went to the front of the room and called on his friends to be seated.

Gnik cleared his throat and began. "In the three weeks since I've moved here, I've made many new friends. Some of you I already know quite well; others, I've just met. Regardless, I wanted to bring you together for a couple of reasons.

"First, I want to thank you all again for taking the time to come here this afternoon and on such short notice. I realize that time is your most valuable resource, and the realization that you're investing an hour or two with me is humbling.

"Next, I'd like to try to express the depth of my gratitude for having met you. Whether it was a chance meeting on the bus or whether we met at a networking event, individually and collectively, you have enriched my life to a degree that you probably don't realize. I am deeply grateful for having met you, and I believe an important part of networking is saying *thank you.*"

As Gnik continued to speak, Pam began to softly hum, "For He's a Jolly Good Fellow." The tune was almost imperceptible at first, but the people seated near Pam picked it up and followed along, until eventually a small chorus filled the restaurant's back room. When Gnik noticed the impromptu musical number, he paused to listen, surprised at the sentiment being expressed. As the song concluded, he smiled bashfully before continuing.

"Finally, I've learned that there is value in bringing people together. It's amazing what can be accomplished with the right group of people!"

Pam stood up and applauded, and the rest of the room quickly followed suit. Gnik smiled and waved his hands, as if to push the attention away from him. When the applause subsided, Pam addressed the group.

"Good afternoon, everyone. My name is Pam … with a P." She winked at Gnik. "I met Gnik the day he moved here, and I have to tell you how far he's come and how impressed I am. The unsure young man I met three weeks ago has become a confident, well-connected *power networker*. Look at what he has brought together after just three weeks. Gnik, this is amazing!"

There was a smattering of applause as Pam continued. "Over the course of the past few weeks, Gnik and I have learned a lot from each other. I have one thing I'd like to share with everyone, something I call the 'HUM philosophy.'" The people in the room looked at each other, wondering where Pam was going with this.

"There's a reason I started humming that song a few minutes ago," she continued. "Did you notice that as I did, people started to fall in, and we all ended up humming and singing the same song? Not only that, but we were in unison. It happens that way almost all the time. Think about the last time, for example, that you were in a group singing 'Happy Birthday.' You probably all started on different notes, but by the end of the song, you were all in one key and in unison.

"HUM is really an acronym. H is for *hear*. You need to hear the people around you. Hear their needs. Listen to them. That's the best way to be sure you're ready to respond to them.

"U is for *understand*. Just hearing your customers, your clients, and your network is not enough. You need to understand them, become fascinated with them, and like them. Understand what they want and need from you and from others.

"And that brings us to M, for *mention* them. It doesn't do a person any good to have you as a network connection if you don't mention his or her name when it could help solve someone else's need. Constantly be on the lookout for ways to solve people's needs, and mention the names of people you know as part of that effort. Be sure to use the eight magic words of networking: I know someone who can get that done."

Pam's smile broadened. "Gnik, let me say again that I'm amazed at how far you've come. Look at this group. You did this. You brought all of us together, and we all have benefitted—or will benefit—as a result." She turned to address the group. "Watch Gnik and do what he's done. It doesn't matter where you are in your own business or in your own network. Gnik is a model for us. After all, there's a little bit of Gnik in each of us."

The group applauded. Gnik stood and embraced Pam, thanking her for being his mentor. The noise subsided, and the group took their seats again, waiting expectantly for Pam to continue.

"Something else I've noticed is how Gnik has been handling his online posts," Pam said. "I don't know if he even realizes he's doing this, and he's still honing the skill, but watch his status updates and blog posts. Gnik has a way of drawing his readers into a conversation. He is creating a dialogue and a community. People love to feel like they belong to something and that they're in on the conversation." She turned back to Gnik. "Keep drawing people into the conversation. You're building something significant."

**Constantly be on the lookout for ways to solve people's needs, and mention the names of people you know as part of that effort. Be sure to use the eight magic words of networking: I know someone who can get that done.**

143

Gnik spoke up. "Thank you, Pam, and thanks to all of you for the lessons you've taught me. It's been a phenomenal few weeks, and I can't wait to share my experiences with my old college crew when I visit my hometown tomorrow. So, thanks again, and please continue to chat and network with one other. I'll look forward to seeing you all at our Gratitude Event next month. It should be fun!"

Garrett stood and lifted his glass. "To connections!"

The group echoed, "To connections!"

The gathering eventually wound down, and Gnik went home to pack for his trip. *I can't wait to tell The Crew what I've learned and share stories about the people I've met*, he thought as, exhausted from the day's activities, he finally climbed into bed and switched off the light.

# Gnik's Aha!

I should implement the "HUM philosophy": Hear and Understand the people I connect with, and then Mention their names to others who can benefit.

# Epilogue

Gnik felt a sense of déjà vu as he entered his hometown coffee shop and took in the familiar surroundings. His thoughts turned to Samantha, one of the original Crew and a close friend. Sam was getting married tomorrow, and some of The Crew who knew Gnik would be in town for the wedding were planning to gather at the coffee shop to hear about his experiences in the city. Word of the reunion had spread quickly via social networks after Gnik created an online event promoting it. He had decided to arrive a little early to get a jump on things. *Being back here feels very strange,* he thought. *What a difference three weeks can make!*

Since he was the first of The Crew to arrive, he claimed an area in the back corner of the shop. A server was wiping the tables nearby; she looked up as Gnik settled into his seat. He smiled, and they exchanged friendly banter until duty called her to the front.

Gnik sipped his coffee and smiled at the memories from his send-off a few short weeks ago. As The Crew began filtering in, his moment of reflection quickly turned to one of reconnection as old friends asked enthusiastically about his new life and chatted about Sam's imminent nuptials. When a lull came in the conversation at last, Gnik stood and addressed his friends.

"Wow," he began. "It doesn't seem possible I've been away for *three whole weeks* already." Laughter rippled across the room. "Really, it's great to be with you again, especially to celebrate Sam's big day."

Gnik's smile broadened. "Three weeks ago, I sat here, a little freaked out, and I listened to you remind me why I had decided to move. There was something important waiting for me in the city. As uncomfortable as I felt, I also knew it would change my life." He heard sounds of agreement. Heads nodded, and eyes expectantly looked to him to continue.

Gnik smiled and took a deep breath. His mind raced, reliving the milestone events of the past few weeks. Gnik's friends seemed to be anticipating some deeply profound insights. "Guys, I told you before that there's nothing special about me—and there's not."

Chad spoke for all. "Even though it's only been three weeks, you're different. I don't mean you're different from us. I mean you're different than you were the last time we met. You seem more sure of yourself. More confident."

In sync, heads around the table nodded in agreement. Gnik heard a couple of his friends ask, "Can you tell us what happened?" Chad opened his hands as if to ask Gnik to explain himself. "What made the difference?"

Gnik pondered the question for a moment, then looked around the room. "When I left, I didn't think I had it in me to be successful at building a network. You all had confidence in me—that helped. I'll share some stories, if you want, but anyone can make this happen. Anyone can increase the size, scope, and quality of their personal network.

"But I don't think it's about meeting people and trading business cards. It's not about being a Facebook friend or having a blog. I've learned some great techniques that I'll share with you to help you make more connections."

Gnik's former college classmates looked at him in anticipation. Gnik didn't break the eye contact he had made with Chad. "Write this down, Chad."

Chad opened a notepad and readied his pen, as if he were about to pounce on the paper. He looked at Gnik and nodded.

"There's so much to explain that I'm not quite sure where to begin. Let me start with some basics. For example, sometimes you may decide to help someone with the expectation that you'll gain some benefit in the end. Don't think like that. Focus on creating a connection. Do things for the joy of doing them. You'll feel better when you don't keep score."

Heads nodded, and Gnik continued. "Focus on the connection, and nurture the relationship. It's not about how many online friends you have. Shift your thinking from 'high tech' to 'high touch.'"

Gnik stopped talking when he realized what he'd said. "Nurture the relationship. I wonder if the connection is secondary to the relationship." He paused, letting his words sink in. "Maybe building the relationship is more important than making the sale. Maybe it's not a contact or a name that we should be going after. Maybe it's the relationship." The Crew looked confused, and a low murmur began to rise.

Gnik sat down in his chair and wiped his forehead with a napkin. "Let me explain how I got to where I am. When I arrived in the city, I went to a coffee shop not much different from this one, and I met a woman named Pam. She became my mentor, and she taught me some things I will never forget."

As he continued his tale, Gnik listened to his own words as if he were hearing them for the first time himself. Then he stopped abruptly, as if he'd hit a brick wall, as it suddenly occurred to him how much more he had to learn about building relationships. *I thought that Pam was an amazing networker, but no—she's a master relationship builder.* He continued by saying, "It's the relationship. That's the secret." He turned his attention back to The Crew. "Building a network is more than shaking hands and trading business cards. It's about building a relationship. Making the sale is secondary."

Gnik said, quietly, almost to himself, "I still have a lot to learn, and I can't wait to get back and see Pam."

Chad was still sitting with his pen poised. "Don't leave us hanging, Gnik. We want to hear everything."

# It's the relationship. That's the secret.

"It's the relationship," Gnik said. "We all want to be connected with people. Then we want those affiliations to become stronger and deeper. We *crave* relationships." Chad was writing furiously.

Gnik continued. "I'll share with you everything I've learned, and it will work for you, too. I'm confident that it will work for you every time." Gnik told The Crew of the daily lessons he'd learned in the city.

Finally Gnik said, "But there's more to it. I've just scratched the surface. Get started with these ideas, and when I visit again, we'll take it to the next level."

And as he wrapped up his story, Gnik smiled and said to himself, *I can't wait to see what's in store when I get back.*

# Gnik's 21 Aha! Moments

We hope you were able to identify—at least a little—with Gnik. We believe there's a little bit of Gnik in each one of us, and it doesn't matter where you're starting from. What matters is taking action. Like Gnik, if you implement these principles of expanding your network, your ability to "know someone who can get that done" will create tremendous opportunities for you to connect with people and solve their problems. Practice one principle each day and see what a difference it makes for you. We'd love to hear your experiences at gnikrowten.com.

For your convenience, following is a complete list of Gnik's 21 Aha! moments:

- Day 1: The act of giving is its own reward. Giving, itself, is a gift to the giver. I can give time, assistance, energy, and resources without the expectation of anything in return.

- Day 2: The Law of Reciprocity: What goes around comes around. If I help others, it is more likely that others will want to help me in return.

- Day 3: When I change how I look at something, then the thing I look at changes.

- Day 4: I can give others the gift of my attention. I should listen twice as much as I speak. When I speak, I learn what I know. When I listen, I learn what others know.

- Day 5: What the other person has to say is more important than what I have to say.

- Day 6: I can leverage online social networks to increase opportunities to connect with others.

- Day 7: Great questions affirm the other person's value. Rather than focus on questions that recall knowledge, I should ask questions that affirm value.

- Day 8: I need to constantly feed my mind and my network. There is no substitute for facts, information, knowledge, and connections.

- Day 9: The bottom line of networking is being visible. I must be seen, heard, and noticed in order to have the success I desire.

- Day 10: My network isn't only people I know or who know me. It includes all the people and talent I have access to.

- Day 11: People aren't offended when I assert myself positively. If I am rejected, it only means that there's not a need for my services right now. Not everything others do is because of me.

- Day 12: Being genuinely interested in people makes them feel important and is the fastest way to build strong business and personal connections.

- Day 13: Most people are more interested in themselves than in me. I need to give a memorable 47-second intro and follow it with, "That's enough about me. What can I do to help you?"

- Day 14: It's amazing what can get done when the right group of people come together.

- Day 15: I will approach my day with a plan. I will find success as I decide what I want to accomplish and then look for opportunities to move in that direction.

- Day 16: There's no shortage of people I can count on or that I can help. As I grow my personal flow of business, my network will grow, and my business will benefit.

- Day 17: Following up with everyone I meet is a powerful way to formalize relationships and build a better network.

- Day 18: When I interact with people, I can turn an unremarkable experience into a memorable one by acting as the host. I want to make sure their needs are being met.

- Day 19: When I become fascinated with other people and listen intently, I get to enjoy the interaction.

- Day 20: When I listen—*really* listen to the other person's story, the whole story—that person will listen more carefully to what I have to say *and* take it more seriously.

- Day 21: I should implement the "HUM philosophy": Hear and Understand the people I connect with, and then Mention their names to others who can benefit.

# About the Authors

**Ron Sukenick** is considered one of America's leading authorities on the topic of networking and business relationship strategies. He is the president and founder of the Relationship Strategies Institute, a global training and business development company that provides the business community with strategies for developing and effectively utilizing deeper professional relationships. He is a dynamic presenter, an intuitive business coach, an expert consultant, and a successful author. His presentations on relationship collaboration and transformation deliver practical information, humor, and immediate results.

Ron's work consistently focuses on the areas of personal and professional relationship success, and he has extensive insight into the processes that connect people to people. He shows his clients how to transcend the standard networking practices to build more authentic and mutually beneficial relationships that enhance the bottom line. He has helped countless companies improve their internal relationships as well as develop and improve critical relationships with clients, vendors, and others outside the company.

Here are a few of Ron's accomplishments:

- Author, *Networking Your Way to Success* (Kendall Hunt, 1995)

- Co-author, *The Power Is In the Connection: Taking Your Personal and Professional Relationships to the Next Level* (self-published, 2004)

- Contributing author, *Masters of Networking*, a *New York Times* best-seller (Bard Press, 2000)

Ron is a highly recognized speaker and trainer who gives programs for corporations, organizations, and associations. His presentations are known for practical information, humor, and results. For further information, please communicate your interest to Ron at rs@ronsukenick.com.

**Ken Williams** is an emerging speaker with a dynamic history of teaching, coaching, and training teams to achieve success. As a sales manager in direct sales and insurance industries, he recruited and trained sales agents, and learned the importance of creating and maintaining relationships. During his corporate career, Ken has worked in customer service as well as in human resources. He has learned the importance of developing business relationships and associations that are mutually beneficial.

A forward-thinking professional, Ken has collaborated with business professionals in diverse organizations to offer his experience and expertise in improving processes, training and mentoring personnel, and improving customer service and relationships. Ken realized his passion for speaking and mentoring when he joined Toastmasters in 2008, and he achieved the designation of Distinguished Toastmaster just 3 years later.

Ken is an exceptional communicator in individual and group settings, and he is sought after for business and creative writing. Ken is currently building his own local marketing business in the Indianapolis area. He can be reached at ken@loyaltymarketingindy.com. This is Ken's first published book.

# More Great Books from Information Today, Inc.

## Face2Face

Using Facebok, Twitter, and Other Social Media Tools to Creat Great Customer Connections

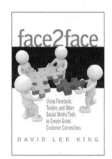

### By David Lee King

With *Face2Face*, David Lee King (*Designing the Digital Experience*) presents a practical guide for any organization that aspires to create deep, direct, and rewarding relationships with patrons and prospects. Going far beyond Facebook and Twitter, King demonstrates how a range of Web 2.0 tools and techniques can be used to start and sustain conversations and humanize the organization in the eyes of those it seeks to serve. He uses real-world examples to illustrate the do's and don'ts of responding to criticism, and explains why and how listening, tone, human-centered site design, and measuring results are all critical components of any customer engagement strategy.

**216 pp/softbound/ISBN 978-0-910965-99-6  $24.95**

## Teach Beyond Your Reach, 2nd Edition

An Instructor's Guide to Developing and Running Successful Distance Learning Classes, Workshops, Training Sessions, and More

### By Robin Neidorf

In this expanded new edition, Robin Neidorf takes a practical, curriculum-focused approach designed to help distance educators develop and deliver courses and training sessions. She shares best practices, surveys the tools of the trade, and covers such key issues as instructional design, course craft, adult learning styles, student-teacher interaction, and learning communities.

**248 pp/softbound/ISBN 978-1-937290-01-6  $29.95**

# Global Mobile

Applications and Innovations for the
Worldwide Mobile Ecosystem

*Edited by Peter A. Bruck and
Madanmohan Rao*

*Global Mobile* examines the foundations of the
worldwide mobile ecosystem through an array of
case studies and perspectives on how mobile is
transforming human enterprise—from business and
healthcare to education, employment,
entertainment, government, and the media.
Contributors describe how mobile can and is being
used to expand economies, alliances, and partnerships, and assess legal,
policy, and regulatory issues and challenges. Combining broad practical
coverage with a pioneering vision, *Global Mobile* is the first essential guide
to the worldwide mobile ecosystem.

**632 pp/softbound/ISBN 978-1-57387-462-5   $49.50**

# The Mobile Marketing Handbook, 2nd Edition

A Step-by-Step Guide to Creating Dynamic Mobile
Marketing Campaigns

*By Kim Dushinski*

In this new interactive edition of her bestselling guide
to mobile marketing, Kim Dushinski shows how any
firm can create successful mobile campaigns without
breaking the bank. Her easy-to-follow advice helps
readers interact with mobile users, build stronger
customer relationships, reach a virtually unlimited
number of new prospects, and gain competitive
advantage by making the move to mobile *now.*

**248 pp/softbound/ISBN 978-0-910965-80-3   $29.95**

# The Internet Book of Life

Use the Web to Grow Richer, Smarter, Healthier, and Happier

### By Irene E. McDermott

No matter what you want to accomplish in life, there are quality, free online resources available to help—if you only had the time to find and evaluate them all! Irene McDermott rides to the rescue with *The Internet Book of Life*—a handy guide to websites, blogs, online tools, and mobile apps. From matters of personal finance to parenting, relationships, health and medicine, careers, travel, hobbies, pets, home improvement, and more, each chapter addresses real-life goals, dilemmas, and solutions. *The Internet Book of Life*—along with its supporting blog—is the lively, indispensable reference that belongs next to every home computer.

320 pp/softbound/ISBN 978-0-910965-89-7 $19.95

# Dancing With Digital Natives

Staying in Step With the Generation That's Transforming the Way Business Is Done

### Edited by Michelle Manafy and Heidi Gautschi

Generational differences have always influenced how business is done, but in the case of digital natives—those immersed in digital technology from birth—we are witnessing a tectonic shift. As an always connected, socially networked generation increasingly dominates business and society, organizations can ignore the implications only at the risk of irrelevance. In this fascinating book, Michelle Manafy, Heidi Gautschi, and a stellar assemblage of experts from business and academia provide vital insights into the characteristics of this transformative generation. Here is an in-depth look at how digital natives work, shop, play, and learn, along with practical advice geared to help managers, marketers, coworkers, and educators maximize their interactions and create environments where everyone wins.

408 pp/hardbound/ISBN 978-0-910965-87-3 $27.95

# True Crime Online
Shocking Stories of Scamming, Stalking,
Murder, and Mayhem

### By J. A. Hitchcock

This new book by a top cybercrime expert and
victim's advocate explores horrific real-life crimes with
roots in cyberspace. Author J. A. Hitchcock (*Net
Crimes & Misdemeanors*) is celebrated for her work to
pass tough cybercrime legislation, train law
enforcement personnel, and help victims fight back.
In *True Crime Online*, she journeys into the darkest
recesses of the internet to document the most
depraved criminals imaginable, from bullies and stalkers to scam artists,
sexual predators, and serial killers. You'll never think about your online
"friends" the same way again!

**176 pp/softbound/ISBN 978-1-937290-00-9   $14.95**


# Web of Deceit
Misinformation and Manipulation in the
Age of Social Media

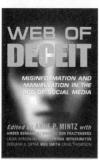

### Edited by Anne P. Mintz

For all its amazing benefits, the worldwide social
media phenomenon—epitomized by such sites and
tools as Facebook, Myspace, eBay, Twitter, and
Craigslist—has provided manipulative people and
organizations with the tools (and human targets) that
allow hoaxes and con games to be perpetrated on a
vast scale. In this eye-opening follow-up to her
popular 2002 book, *Web of Deception*, Anne P. Mintz
brings together a team of expert researchers, journalists, and subject
experts to explain how misinformation is intentionally spread and to
illuminate the dangers in a range of critical areas. *Web of Deceit* is a
must-read for any internet user who wants to avoid being victimized by
liars, thieves, and propagandists in the age of ubiquitous social media.

**224 pp/softbound/ISBN 978-0-910965-91-0   $29.95**

# Excellence Every Day

Make the Daily Choice—Inspire Your Employees and Amaze Your Customers

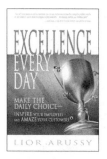

### By Lior Arussy

If mediocre performance or results are acceptable at any level within your organization, this may be the most important book you will read this year. Lior Arussy explores and offers a solution to the root problem that keeps firms from delighting customers and inspiring superior performance and job satisfaction among employees. The "Excellence Myth" is a subtle yet pervasive mindset that undermines individual performance, erodes customer loyalty, and erases any competitive advantage a firm may enjoy or hope to gain. Arussy's inspired (and inspiring) remedy is the "Daily Choice," a strategy that empowers employees to reach new heights of excellence—creating delightful customer experiences and achieving superior results from the bottom up.

**240 pp/softbound/ISBN 978-0-910965-79-8   $24.95**

# The Extreme Searcher's Internet Handbook, 4th Edition

A Guide for the Serious Searcher

### By Randolph Hock

*The Extreme Searcher's Internet Handbook* is the essential guide for anyone who uses the internet for research—librarians, teachers, students, writers, business professionals, and others who need to search the web proficiently. In this fully updated fourth edition, Ran Hock covers strategies and tools for all major areas of internet content. Readers with little to moderate searching experience will appreciate Hock's helpful, easy-to-follow advice, while experienced searchers will discover a wealth of new ideas, techniques, and resources.

**344 pp/softbound/ISBN 978-1-937290-02-3  $24.95**

# Point, Click, and Save
## Mashup Mom's Guide to Saving and Making Money Online

### By Rachel Singer Gordon

This immensely practical book and its supporting website provide clear tech-savvy advice to reassure readers who are new to the world of saving and earning money online, while providing an array of innovative ideas, strategies, and resources for those who have been clipping coupons (online *or* off) for years. Rachel Singer Gordon is "Mashup Mom"—a widely read blogger who combines high- and low-tech strategies to help her readers achieve financial objectives. Here, she helps money-conscious web users gain immediate relief from the pain of rising prices, find fabulous freebies, and much more!

**304 pp/softbound/ISBN 978-0-910965-86-6  $19.95**

# Mob Rule Learning
## Camps, Unconferences, and Trashing the Talking Head

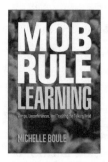

### By Michelle Boule

In this first comprehensive book about the unconference movement, Michelle Boule explains why traditional conferences and learning environments increasingly fail to meet the needs of professionals. She offers a step-by-step approach to planning a camp or unconference, along with case studies, interviews, and examples of emerging education and training models.

**248 pp/softbound/ISBN 978-0-910965-92-7   $24.95**